BLISSFUL WEDDING PLANNING

Congratulations on your engagement Zara.

I hope you find this book useful, insightful and makes your wedding planning..... Blissful.

Happy planning,

BLISSFUL
WEDDING PLANNING
Becoming a Stoic Bride

CHRIS PIERCY

Copyright © 2018 Chris Piercy
Cover design by Steve Rowe
Front cover image by Sadie Osborne
Editing and book design by Ilsa Hawtin

The moral right of the author has been asserted. All rights reserved. This book may not be reproduced in whole or in part without written permission from the author, except by a reviewer who may quote brief passages in a review; nor may any of this book be reproduced, stored in a retrieval system, or transmitted in any form or by any means, electronic, mechanical, photocopying, recording, or other, without written permission from the author.

Author's website: www.chrispiercymagic.co.uk

ISBN 978-1-73-157979-9

To Natalie, for standing by me through everything we've been through and always believing in me.

To my daughters, Sienna and India, for making me laugh every day and reminding me what's important.

To the rest of my family, for their unerring support with all my business ventures.

And finally, to everyone I've ever known. I've learnt something from each and every one of you, which has helped me grow as a person.

"We all love ourselves more than other people, but care more about their opinions than our own."

Marcus Aurelius

~

"We have control over when, how, and where to plant a seed, not over what it will become."

Mokokoma Mokhonoana

Contents

Foreword	xi
Why I'm writing this book	1
A bit about me	5
What the hell is Stoicism?	9
Chapter 1: The power of gratitude	13
Chapter 2: Understanding control	33
Chapter 3: Wanting and needing	75
Chapter 4: Giving permission	109
Chapter 5: Amor fati	135
Chapter 6: Being the gatekeeper	159
Chapter 7: Remembering we're all human	191
Chapter 8: Storytelling	217
Epilogue: Becoming a Stoic Bride	235
Acknowledgements	237

Foreword

It's often said that the best therapists and coaches apply the principles they learn to themselves. I fondly remember my time in training as one of the most condensed periods of personal transformation I ever experienced. I was hit by "Aha!" moment after "Aha!" moment, as I realised that these poor neurotic clients we spoke about in the classroom could easily have been me!

Self-help concepts glibly presented in memes on social media feeds were explained, the science behind them examined, ancient philosophies underpinning modern therapeutic principles road-tested.

The difference, I discovered, between reading a meme about gratitude, and living from a place of appreciation, tranquillity and contentment, is the practice of these ideas, and the know-how to actually implement them. Inspiration is worthless without the tools to use and become what has moved you.

In your hands, right now, you are holding these tools.

I met Chris years ago when he was a therapy student. Strikingly adroit with the subject matter, he became a capable therapist unreasonably quickly. I asked him if he had studied before, and soon enough realised there was a polymath in our midst: part-way through a mathematics degree, a hypnotist and magician – he held our conversation while doing things that were definitely impossible with elastic bands, paperclips and other classroom stationery. Perhaps you'd expect someone with such an array of talent to be egotistic or recognition-hungry, but he is annoyingly humble and – perhaps the thing that speaks loudest of all – he is incredibly kind, warm-hearted and real.

The world of therapy scored a win!

And then a loss.

Chris's magic career took off to the extent where he could not maintain his therapy practice. I have seen first-hand how he took all he learned during his training, applied it to himself, and how he continues to grow as an exceptional human being and elite professional. If only he would come back to practising therapy! Imagine how many hundreds of people he could help with his knowledge!

Then he told me he was writing this book. I couldn't be happier to endorse it. Inside these covers are pages and pages of your own "Aha!" moments, just waiting for you, plus all the tools you could need to make these ideas part of your daily life.

Read it, do the exercises in it, and your life will change immeasurably for the better.

Lucy Angel Hyde
Professional Life Coach, Hypnotherapist, Warrior

Why I'm writing this book

There are countless reasons that wedding planning is considered to be stressful. While I prefer to avoid generalisations, let alone sexist generalisations, I think I can safely say that a lot of women harbour aspirations of creating a perfect wedding day and feel stressed about not getting it right. Let's get this straight from the start: I don't criticise anyone in the slightest for wanting their wedding to be perfect or feeling stressed about it. It's almost inevitable, under the circumstances in our society, that so many people feel those pressures.

But does it really need to be stressful to plan a wedding and get through the day?

NO.

There are many reasons why you might right now be laughing at that statement. They're the same reasons that weddings are "known" to be stressful, including the feeling of being in the spotlight from the moment you get engaged, the outpourings from social media and magazines on everyone else's apparently perfect wedding, precedents that have been set by weddings you've attended, or even pressures stemming from your own personality and/or social standing. Your life felt busy enough before, but now you're suddenly faced with hundreds of new choices from an infinite list of sources and options. Overnight, you have to master a plethora of tasks, including careful budgeting, deciding on a date, finding a venue, choosing wedding favours that everyone will remember . . . the list is endless. All this for an event you've never planned before, and the final straw: you've heard a million times how stressful it is to plan a wedding.

I'm writing this book because I genuinely want to help as many brides-to-be as possible to beat the system, love every minute of planning their wedding, and enjoy every second of their very special day. I'm going to reveal simple and straightforward techniques and explanations, which will enable you to become the bride that everyone envies. It's likely that you will be the only woman they know who doesn't moan and fret about all the pressures involved, and it's even more likely that your wedding will be the one that everyone enjoys and remembers the most. You will have become the Stoic Bride.

I need to ask you first to make a conscious decision to banish any doubts caused by my gender or vocation ("How can this bloke – a magician – tell me how to plan my wedding?!"). I'll tell you more about my background in the next chapter, but in short: my work brings me into daily contact with anything and everything to do with weddings. I've been lucky to meet hundreds of brides-to-be, in different phases of stress and excitement about their nuptials, and I attend one or two weddings nearly every weekend due to my work as a magician. I am a qualified and experienced hypnotherapist, and a scholar and everyday practiser of Stoic philosophy. Don't worry about the philosophy thing – it won't be boring and you won't have to study anything. You'll only need to absorb and practise some easy techniques, which will help you to relax and thoroughly enjoy your wedding and all the preparations.

Becoming a Stoic Bride will not only remove pressures from social expectations, it will allow you to plan a wedding that is true both to yourself and to your partner. This will be completely free (excluding the cost of this book), it won't conflict with any religious beliefs and you won't need to change your personality or your style of wedding. You'll only have to put in some time and mental energy, but you'll gain more time and energy in return. Best of all, you will be able to relax while planning your wedding and thoroughly enjoy your big day.

Please don't feel overwhelmed by the prospect of changing your mindset and challenging every preconception you may have about weddings! It might be as easy as only reading this book and allowing your mind to change all on its own. And the very techniques I give you will make it easier for you not to feel overwhelmed – by anything. However receptive your mind is to the positive changes in this book, it's inevitable that you will get better and better at all the techniques as you continue to practise them. But you don't need to master any or all of them before you start even thinking about planning your wedding – they will start helping you straight away, whatever stage you are at.

Don't worry if you don't have time to read everything in one go. Start with these short (but vital) introductions, then read the first chapter on the power of gratitude. Even if that was the only chapter you then integrated into your life, your life would definitely become richer because of it. And I feel confident that the positive effects you start to enjoy will make you *long* to read more, to start experiencing all the other benefits.

Here's the hidden perk to this book – the free, no-strings-attached prize, which won't have been obvious until now: this book isn't only about wedding planning. Everything I cover will help you to become more content with your life, more confident in yourself, more grounded and more capable of achieving anything you want. There you go – proof that you can't judge a book by its cover.

I personally always find it easier to have trust in someone I know something about, so I'm going to start with a short description about me and my background.

A bit about me

I am a professional magician, based in Dorset on the south coast of the UK. I live with my partner, Natalie, and our two daughters, Sienna and India.

Around 70–80% of my work as a magician comes from weddings. At the time of writing, I have worked for eight years as a professional magician. I've performed at hundreds of weddings, from very small and intimate days right up to lavish 200-guest castle weddings, some of which have cost probably in excess of £100,000. I'm extremely proud to say that I am now recommended by venues that are at the highest end of the market here in Dorset, as they have witnessed time and again the value that I add, namely in improving the smooth running of wedding days, and increasing the levels of enjoyment of the wedding couple and all their guests. I'm extremely lucky in that I love performing magic, and can't think of an event I would prefer to work at than a couple's incredibly special day – the day they celebrate their love and make a lifelong commitment to each other.

You might still be wondering why on earth you're reading a book written by a magician about how to be a calm and happy bride. If I were in your shoes, I'm sure I'd be asking the same thing. I'm sure you'd be asking me to take your shoes off before I broke them, too.

In short, the reason I am writing this book is because it brings together three of my very favourite things:

1. Weddings
2. Stoic philosophy
3. Helping people become happier

Having already talked about my connection to weddings, I'll now touch on the second point. The following chapter will tell you a little bit more about Stoic philosophy, but let's start with how I got into it.

Around six years ago I decided to add hypnosis to my performances, alongside the close-up magic and mind reading I performed. I began learning the process of how to hypnotise people, to get them to do incredible things such as being convinced their hands were stuck to tables, forgetting their names or believing that I was Tom Hardy. Having realised the power of hypnosis as an entertainment medium, and that I had some talent for it, I decided to also try and use my skills for a greater good and so trained to be a hypnotherapist. This tied in nicely with the third point above, that I genuinely like to try and make people happier.

In January 2015 I received my Hypnotherapist's Practitioner Diploma, as well as qualifications in cognitive behavioural therapy (CBT) and neuro-linguistic programming (NLP). As with any therapy, it is vital that skills are kept current and up to date through continuous professional development, so I made a deliberate commitment to attend additional training courses every few months.

It was at one of these training sessions that my hypnotherapy tutor, Adam Eason, gave a talk on Stoicism, also recommending a book. From that day, I was hooked. In fact, there was one quote, which Adam included in his presentation, which was the real game changer for me. That quote is now my very favourite and one that I try to live my life by. When I'm at my happiest, I find that I'm living by this perfectly. Whenever I'm less happy, it's because I'm not following it.

> "Do not spoil what you have by desiring what you have not. What you have now was once among that which you desired."
>
> Epicurus

For me that's really powerful stuff, which I find incredibly grounding.

Stoicism has already had an immense impact on my life. I don't consider myself to be the perfect Stoic, but I don't consider that goal as an achievement to be ticked off a list – it's an ongoing journey of life improvement.

I began combining Stoic teachings with hypnotherapy when helping all my clients, and the results were compelling. Whether they came to me with crippling depression or a fear of eating anything other than chicken nuggets – or anything in between – Stoicism compounded the many beneficial effects of hypnotherapy. Stoicism can help absolutely anyone in this world to become more grounded and achieve a more helpful mindset, improving their satisfaction in life, while also finding solutions for any issues they are facing.

Unfortunately – or fortunately, depending on how you look at it – my magic business began to skyrocket at the time I started my own hypnotherapy business. Within 18 months I simply did not have the time to see hypnotherapy clients alongside my magic business as well as my family commitments. I was also studying for an Open University maths degree (yes, I barely had time to sleep!).

I closed my hypnotherapy business in 2016, but I remained fully committed to continuing to live as Stoically as possible. I also remained fully committed to helping people, which has now given me the motivation to write this book. I sincerely hope that you enjoy it, and that you gain a new and more positive perspective towards planning your wedding, the day itself, and even the rest of your life.

What the hell is Stoicism?

You might be wondering why you have to learn anything about any type of philosophy in order to be able to enjoy planning your wedding. Rest assured, this isn't going to be a history lesson and you're not going to have to study anything or take any tests. This brief chapter will give you solid straightforward understanding about something I have studied in depth, which has helped me become happier with just about everything in my life. You don't need to read any further on the subject, although it's very possible you might be intrigued enough by the positive effects you start experiencing that you decide at some point to learn more about Stoicism. For now, you can simply read this book and start to enjoy the beneficial changes.

A misnomer?

A lot of people reading the word "stoic" will search for the word in their own mental dictionary and find a definition meaning emotionless, resilient or brave. A stoic is often defined as someone who is unable or unwilling to display emotion. Being stoic is sometimes likened to the "very

British" idea of having a stiff upper lip about everything. That is very different from what we're talking about here. You might notice the change now to a capital "s" when referring to anything related to Stoic philosophy, rather than the standard, everyday understanding of stoicism.

This book is about understanding the fulfilling aspects of Stoicism. It's not heavy or boring, and it isn't going to require hours of meditation or perseverance. By absorbing some very basic principles of Stoic philosophy, you will be able to start to develop a new mindset, and to enjoy some dramatic and positive effects on your life.

Possibly the briefest summary in the world about Stoicism

Stoicism is one of the ancient schools of philosophy, founded in Ancient Greece by Zeno of Citium in the 3rd Century BC. It doesn't assert any strange or complicated theories, and it's probably the simplest type of philosophy to understand.

In short, Stoicism asks us to concern ourselves only with those things that we can actually control, namely our thoughts and our actions, and as such not to allow external events to spoil our happiness. It asks us to view the world as it genuinely is – unpredictable – and to acknowledge that our time on the planet is fleeting, in the grand scheme of things, inspiring us to make the most of our lives rather than feel depressed that we won't be around for ever. Finally, Stoicism teaches us that the source of dissatisfaction within our lives comes from our dependency on making impulsive, emotional decisions, rather than allowing logic to dictate our choices.

Stoicism has had some very prominent devotees, none greater than Marcus Aurelius, who was a Roman emperor and therefore the most powerful man in the world at that time. Despite his elevated position, Aurelius remained grounded throughout his life, writing a diary of his thoughts on a daily basis in order to remain Stoical. The diary has been translated into a book, *Meditations*, which I recommend you read one day if you wish to take your Stoical practices further.

Now, let's start with how following just a few basic principles of Stoicism can make a significant difference to how much you can really relax and enjoy your wedding planning.

Tranquillity

Anyone who has mastered Stoic philosophy is said to have achieved "tranquillity", a state in which all negative emotions have been removed. The person can remain unperturbed by outside actions and events, and feel perfectly happy, knowing that they only ever control their own thoughts and actions.

If you follow the few exercises in this book, after embracing the ideas I give you about Stoicism, you will start to experience your own levels of tranquillity. Imagine now that you will soon have just the same things going on in your life, but you simply won't bother feeling stressed about them. You'll find yourself being much less self-critical, and no longer fret about what other people are saying or thinking. It's almost inevitable that you'll be sleeping better and feeling like you have more energy, both of which help you to feel more creative and relaxed. You'll realise that you used to feel an overwhelming amount of pressure to create the perfect wedding . . . but now it all just feels like an enjoyable few months where you can spoil yourself and plan what you know is going to be a beautiful day with your close friends and family.

Doesn't that sound ideal?

Does it sound like the perfect mindset for your wedding planning?

It's time for you to learn how you can become a Stoic Bride.

CHAPTER 1
The power of gratitude

> "The happiest people are not those who have the most, but those who are the most grateful for what they have."
>
> Mokokoma Mokhonoana

Your life is pretty bloody close to perfect right now. Yes, I'm speaking to all of you right now – every single reader.

YOUR life is pretty close to perfect.

It's likely that you've found that a jarring statement. You might now be feeling defensive, like you're on the back foot. You *know* your life could be so much better than it is right now – who does this moron magician think he is, coming along telling you that your life is pretty close to perfect?

How dare I say that? I don't know you. I don't know what you've had to do to get where you are, or what you have to go through on a daily basis. Maybe your life sometimes feels like hell?

If that statement upset you, or maybe even made you want to put this book down, then this is exactly the book you need to read. We have some work to do together.

Let's look at this from a completely different angle.

Real gratitude

In August 2005, Hurricane Katrina passed just south east of New Orleans. The devastation it caused was catastrophic, with damage estimated at over $100 billion USD. More devastating than any financial ruin was that more than 1,500 people lost their lives.

Homes were ripped apart, buildings were flattened, infrastructure was utterly destroyed. Some people lost everything they had. They were trapped, they were injured; and if they were among the lucky ones that were rescued, how did they feel and react?

The answer to that question: happy. Actually, "happy" doesn't even begin to cover it – they said they were elated, ecstatic and overjoyed. People who owned only the clothes they were wearing were crying tears of happiness just to be alive. They didn't know where their next meal or their next drink of clean water was coming from, or where they were going to sleep that night. They just knew that they were alive, and that was enough to make them feel incredibly happy.

You will never meet a more grateful person than someone who has lost everything yet still has their life. This is gratitude at its purest and most concentrated form.

If I now repeat my statement from the start of this chapter, that your life is pretty close to perfect, I'm sure you won't find it as audacious. This is all about perspective.

I do get it – in those moments where everything is lost and all you have is your life, it's a lot easier to be grateful for it because it is all you have. I would love you, though, to imagine how powerful and grounding it would be for you if you could feel that grateful for all the truly incredible things you have in your life, all the time.

Everyday gratitude

Gratitude is one of the pillar concepts within Stoic philosophy and I genuinely wish it was a pillar of modern society too. Sadly, the truth is that gratitude isn't even a single stone in the foundations of a pillar of our society, let alone a pillar itself.

There is an obsession nowadays about having the next big thing. It's about status, one-upmanship and keeping up with the Joneses (or the Kardashians). Modern society is essentially about never being allowed to be 100% happy with where you are right here and right now. Magazines tell us what we should be wearing and newspapers what we should be thinking. YouTubers show us what we should be doing. And social media gives a large proportion of our society the (generally false) impression that *everyone* else is happier with *everything* that's happening in their lives.

I can think of only one form of marketing that celebrates physical differences and self-confidence: the Dove Campaign for Real Beauty. Dove's advertising strategy, to empower women and banish self-doubt, was so different from any other campaign that it won numerous ad awards and led to vastly improved brand awareness and sales. Sadly, though, this advertising strategy was not emulated by many other businesses.

We are all surrounded by adverts just about every second of our waking lives. In newspapers and magazines, on shopping boards, television, websites, billboards, t-shirts, packaging and coffee cups. Unless you are reading this on a beach or up a mountain, I bet you can spot umpteen forms of advertising just by glancing around you. Here's the important point: how many of those adverts tell us, "You know what? You look great exactly as you are, and you can be happy with everything you have and all that you do. In fact, keep everything exactly the same, unless YOU decide on your own terms that a change needs to be made"?

CHAPTER 1 – THE POWER OF GRATITUDE

Dove's success came only from reversing the trend, from its advertising standing out as different. Generally speaking, positive advertising sadly doesn't sell products.

Perfect Stoic gratitude comes from reversing the trend for yourself. It's about looking at yourself in the mirror (metaphorically and/or literally) and saying to yourself, candidly, that you are content with everything in your life – how you look, what you're doing, what you own – everything.

If you have felt any criticism from reading about how you should feel more grateful in life, please also reverse that feeling. There is no "should" here. You haven't done anything wrong, and I'm not telling you that you haven't shown enough gratitude to anyone else. This is all about learning to experience enhanced levels of gratitude in your own mind, purely for your own personal benefit.

What are you grateful for?

What is the first thing that comes into your head when you think about what you are grateful for? Please answer that question to yourself now. Take a moment and think about it for a few minutes or, even better, write down a list of the first few things that pop into your head.

Read on only after you have made that list, whether in your mind or on paper . . .

Answers will vary massively, depending on endless different factors. There's no right or wrong answer here. Actually, all answers are right because our end goal is being grateful for everything.

Perhaps you've written down that you're grateful for having met the person you're going to marry. Maybe you've thought about that situation more specifically, for example about how grateful you are that your partner makes a real effort to get on with your friends. Or maybe you've thought about all the finer details, including how grateful you are that they always take the rubbish out because they know how much you hate doing it.

You might have thought about how grateful you are to your parents for the upbringing they gave you and for how much support they still provide. You might be appreciating how your dad is always at the end of the phone, ready to come round with a drill when your latest DIY attempt has failed.

Like I said, there are no wrong answers.

Maybe your first thought was something more material, such as a car, a house, or the fact that you can afford cool gadgets. I did say there were no wrong answers, but if you've thought of something like this, then it might fall into the category of "less right answers".

Elevating your gratitude

Gratitude can be taken to extremes in terms of how you define it, what you're grateful for and how grateful you are for it.

An optimist talks about a glass being half-full.

A pessimist would say it is half-empty.

A good Stoic might talk about how grateful he is even to have any water. He may go further and talk about how grateful he is to have a glass. He might even say how grateful he is that there is a substance that can not only be crafted into a shape that allows liquid to be held in it, but that it is also transparent, so that he can see the contents of the vessel!

You could even now think about how grateful you could choose to feel about being able to read and understand these words.

Gratitude and your wedding planning

If you're marrying someone that you have had an absolutely free choice in marrying, then hopefully you've already begun to realise how grateful you can feel to be in that situation. Or consider the utter beauty of the fact that you have found someone to spend the rest of your life with, and not only do you love them, but that love is reciprocated. Even without a wedding, that is something ridiculously special that needs to be deeply treasured and never, ever taken for granted.

Think about all the things you are considering including to make up your wedding day – the venue, the flowers, the food, the entertainment, the photographer, the guests, and so much more. Recognising all of those things as sources of immense gratitude will only help you to feel better about everything.

By understanding the fortunate position you are in and being grateful for everything you have at your wedding, you will be able to look at what you're creating and be pleased with it, which in turn will reduce any feelings of stress if anything doesn't go exactly to plan.

Being grateful is the exact opposite of taking things for granted. When you take things for granted, you don't have the respect and appreciation for what those things are and, more specifically, how they will help to improve your life, including your wedding day. This in turn means that, if anything goes wrong, you'll be left feeling disappointed or upset, along with a stack of other things you have no respect for.

By adopting the Stoical approach to gratitude within your wedding planning, if for some really odd reason everything went horribly wrong and all your suppliers cancelled, you'd still be in the enviable situation where you'd be happily grateful just to have the people you love around you. (That's not to say you're not allowed to feel angry at all your suppliers for cancelling on you – I'll come back to that in the final three chapters of this book.)

Consider another scenario where, in the month before the wedding, you find that – shock horror – you've come in under budget and have £500 to spend on something else for the day! So you decide to go crazy and book, say, a photobooth, only to feel stressed when you find they are all booked up because you're getting married on a Saturday in July. Rather than feeling angry at how you now cannot have a photobooth, it would instead be much better Stoic practice to be grateful for:

- Even getting married in the first place
- Now having £500 to spend on something other than a photobooth
- Having £500 SPARE, whereas you could be scraping by from payday to payday

One of the fundamental elements of Stoicism is to truly understand that happiness and tranquillity come from how we decide to react to circumstances beyond our control, and remaining grateful for all that we have.

Becoming grateful

"But Chris," I hear you cry, "I know how lucky I am to have these things."

Well, that's fantastic. Now I'm going to give you a couple of easy exercises to prove it to yourself. Hey, I'm not the one that you have to convince.

EXERCISE 1
GRATITUDE LISTS

During my time working as a hypnotherapist, this exercise was something I requested of every single one of my clients, starting after our very first session together. I've adapted this to wedding planning, just as I would have adapted it to any client's specific source of anxiety.

The idea of this exercise is about as simple as it gets, but do not allow its simplicity to fool you. It comes in two parts:

1. Every day write down one thing about your wedding that you're grateful for

2. Every day reread everything you've put onto the list, and then add something new to it

Like I said, this is about as simple as it gets, or at least it is for the first few weeks. I'm sure you could easily reel off a whole bunch of things to be grateful for about your wedding, especially as the last few minutes of reading have primed you for this.

Once you've completed your list for a month, you'll have 30 things on your list and you'll still have to think of more things to be grateful for. Two months in, you'll be up to 60 and you'll still have to keep going. It's at this stage of the exercise that you and your fantastic brain can really get into the nitty-gritty of gratitude, drilling down to the things that were not remotely obvious when you first started your list.

Rereading all the points already on your list will compound the gratitude you felt when you first identified each item, so the positive effects of gratitude will strengthen every day.

Start this right now. All you need is a piece of paper and a pen, or you could keep the list in the notes section of your phone. Write today's entry and then set a reminder to do the same every day at the same time. The ongoing dedication to completing this task each day will solidly ground you and create a genuine sense that you are in an incredibly fortunate situation, preventing you from taking any part of it for granted. As a Stoic Bride, you will understand every single facet of your wedding day, appreciate every single thing and every person, and feel grateful for absolutely all of it.

How to premeditate the evils (that's not a sentence I ever thought I'd write)

Picture this. It's the morning of your wedding but you accidentally drank a little too much last night and woke up feeling awful. You overslept, but that isn't immediately critical because your make-up artist got a puncture driving over so she was late anyway. The bridal hair-stylist team has had two employees come down with norovirus, so there's only one person to do your hair plus your mum and your four bridesmaids. You are told there's only time to do three people, so it's up to you to decide which of the three of your bridesmaids will have to style their own hair. After all that, your photographer somehow manages to drop one of his cameras into a puddle as he's leaving your house, destroying the photos of you getting ready.

It is absolutely tipping down with rain, with a little hail thrown in, even though it's the height of summer and the last few days have seen nothing but glorious sunshine. Your pristine white Rolls Royce arrives 15 minutes late due to traffic; it is also now a distinct browny-beige, as a lorry drenched it with muddy water. The dress you spent a full month's wages on fits perfectly, thanks to the countless fittings you had, but sadly it gets saturated as you walk to the car. Then a bird does a poo on your shoulder. Your chauffeur stinks of whisky and moans that his wife announced yesterday she was leaving him. He has clearly been drinking all night and spends the entire journey to the church telling you how marriage is an utter waste of time.

You arrive at the church 25 minutes late, soaking wet, with the bird poo still on your shoulder. Still in shock from your journey with the drink-driving chauffeur, you walk down the aisle surrounded by those you love and care for, then you marry the love of your life.

Does that all sound a little ridiculous and over the top? Stick with me – there are good reasons for imagining this very bleak scenario. The story is an example of negative visualisation. Marcus Aurelius had an infinitely more awesome name for it: *premeditatio malorum* (premeditation of evils).

There's a good chance, especially if you're someone who suffers with anxiety, that you're wondering why on earth you'd want to deliberately imagine this or any other horrendous story – isn't it only going to make you uncomfortable and anxious? Well, yes; and that might not necessarily be a bad thing. The feelings will be temporary, and the positive after-effects will far outweigh any initial anxiety. I'm even going to give you a simple exercise now to exacerbate the initial negativity and make it much more personal.

EXERCISE 2
NEGATIVE VISUALISATION

You might be happy to keep your eyes closed, as suggested below, for this exercise. However, please don't feel you have to if that is difficult or uncomfortable in any way – you will still gain from the exercise if you follow it with your eyes open.

If you are happy to shut your eyes, you can simply read through the whole exercise a couple of times before starting, to memorise the steps (don't worry – the steps are logical and easy to remember). Or, if or when you are somewhere you can listen in peace to an audio recording, go to www.chrispiercymagic.co.uk/bwp-exercises to hear my extended explanation and recording of this exercise, which will be even easier to follow and more effective.

- Find somewhere quiet where you're not going to be disturbed

- Sit down, make yourself comfortable and close your eyes

- Concentrate on your breathing. Don't try to change or control it – just be aware of the breath entering and leaving your body

If you find yourself distracted – say, by a sound or a new thought that crosses your mind – that's fine. Don't beat yourself up; just acknowledge the distraction then bring your concentration back to your breathing. You will now be approaching the best mindset in order to visualise for this exercise.

It's fairly likely that you have already imagined a picture-perfect image of how your wedding would ideally be. I would now like you to:

- Visualise this perfect day in your head, thinking about the different parts of the day – the people, the weather, the venue – anything and everything you've already thought about or planned

- Next, imagine that you're removing every single thing you've organised for your big day, one by one. For example, imagine that the florist doesn't deliver the flowers. Picture the make-up artist not turning up. Add in a scenario where somehow you end up getting married in jeans and a t-shirt. Take away every lovely thing and imagine how your wedding would then be

- Do this until you're left with just you, together with your partner, getting married

- Now imagine your life without your partner in it

- Spend a few minutes visualising all of this until that final, sad image is firmly locked into your mind

(Sorry, this all feels pretty bleak, but you're also very aware that none of that is actually going to happen.)

Next up a cliché: "You don't know what you've got until it is gone". How many times have you been told that? How many times have you been reminded of that saying when you've experienced a loss of some sort?

By allowing yourself to visualise this horrible scenario of everything going wrong on your wedding day, you accomplish a great number of things. By truly understanding how your wedding or your life would be with something important missing, you will garner a genuine hold on exactly what that thing means to you. Once you appreciate how it would feel to lose something, you can truly understand how much it means to you, which gives you real gratitude for that thing. You will naturally no longer take it for granted, instead treating it with respect and appreciation. Nothing will make you love something more than fully appreciating what it would be like not to have it in your life.

The Stoics would even muse upon the loss of their children to make sure that they appreciated them fully and loved them unconditionally. You might not feel the need to take your own visualisation quite as far, although it could be helpful at times. The next time your kids are driving you up the wall and you find yourself yearning for your old, unencumbered existence, try taking two minutes away from the situation and actually picturing your life with your children no longer in it. Your gratitude and patience should be immediately restored, at least until your children next play up.

Another enormous benefit to the wedding-specific negative visualisation exercise is that you may suddenly realise that something you've organised feels unnecessary or undesirable. For example, when you imagined the sweet cart supplier cancelling on you at the last minute, you felt pretty indifferent, or even happy about the money you'd be saving. After the exercise, you may well then question why you even wanted a sweet cart – a friend persuaded you it was a must-have, but it doesn't even fit in with the rest of your day. You can then decide against the sweet cart and save that money for something else.

Whether you only feel more grateful for everything you have organised or also decide to ditch a few unnecessary expenses, the exercise will help you realise what is really important to you and your wedding.

Finally, doing this exercise will mentally prepare you for the absolute worst. As such, it will allow you to create potential contingency plans in case any minor disaster strikes. And if anything does go wrong on the day, you'll be too busy feeling happy about everything else to be distressed by the setback.

I'm not suggesting for a second that anticipating every possible thing going wrong is like some crazy magic spell that'll make any real setback perfectly acceptable. But wouldn't you prefer to be prepared for things not running to plan and then find your whole wedding day easier, rather than the other way around?

Conclusion on the power of gratitude

Being genuinely grateful and feeling very fortunate don't quite form the polar opposites of being stressed and unhappy with your situation, but it is near-impossible for feelings of stress and sadness to exist in your mind at the same time as fortune and gratitude. Practising the exercises in this chapter will have given you a great start on the Stoic journey. You can start feeling altogether more positive about planning your wedding, as well as less worried about the prospect of anything not going to plan.

Gratitude is such a simple concept to understand and apply, but it can be a more complicated beast to keep tamed. If or when you earn and achieve more in life, it might become harder to stay true to the principle of gratitude, and easier to slip back into the habit of taking things for granted. But it will be extremely easy for you to at least complete the exercises in this chapter and develop a grateful mindset towards planning your wedding. Hopefully you will then find it easy to employ the same techniques throughout the rest of your life, to give you more appreciation and enjoyment of anything and everything you experience.

Here are some positive declarations about your new mindset, some or all of which you will already have achieved.

Being a Stoic Bride will empower you to:

- Understand the concept and benefits of gratitude
- Take nothing for granted
- Know that you have everything you need
- Feel full of gratitude
- Feel prepared for failure and ready for success

This thorough understanding of gratitude gives a solid foundation for the next important area of Stoicism, which is just as important in helping you to fully enjoy planning your wedding: control. When thinking about control in relation to wedding planning, you'd be forgiven for thinking of a bridezilla dictating instructions to every poor soul involved. Chapter 2 is going to give you a new and very positive take on control, according to Stoic philosophy.

CHAPTER 2
Understanding control

The last time you were worried or anxious about something, I can 99% guarantee it was due to your lack of understanding of control.

That's a bold statement, and one that might sound unfairly critical. Allow me to explain.

Stoics believe that each and every person has their own "sphere of influence". Essentially, your own sphere of influence encompasses all the things in your life over which you have any control. Stoics maintain that ANYTHING outside your sphere of influence should be regarded as an external source of discomfort, which must be ignored and not allowed to affect your tranquillity.

In "What the hell is Stoicism?", I explained how being Stoic is less about not letting any emotions affect you and more about the removal of negative emotions. By learning about your sphere of influence and about what you *actually* control, you will first begin to understand and then put into practice the idea of not letting things outside of your control affect you.

> "God, grant me the serenity to accept the
> things I cannot change,
> Courage to change the things I can,
> And wisdom to know the difference."
>
> 20th Century Christian Serenity Prayer

This is used by Alcoholics Anonymous, and by other 12-step recovery programmes. Regardless of any religious beliefs, the Serenity Prayer forms a solid foundation for the Stoic interpretation of control. If the religious connotation doesn't sit right with you, simply omit the word "God" and address the prayer as a statement to yourself.

The trichotomy of control

As I'm sure you know, "trichotomy" refers to something split into three parts. Control falls into three categories, namely:

1. Things we can control
2. Things we can't control
3. Things that we have some control over

Things we can control

Believe it or not, there are only two things that we can control – our thoughts and our actions. That's it – nothing else whatsoever.

Things we can't control

This list is endless, but I'm going to pick out a few things that I feel are pertinent in relation to your wedding:

- The weather
- People's opinions of you
- What people think
- What people do
- The past

With the exception of the weather, these are all very general things, which I will expand on a little later.

Things that we have some control over

This is often the hardest category to grasp, so I always like to use an analogy or two, to give better understanding.

Analogy 1 – A tennis match

Imagine you and I are playing a lovely game of tennis. A crowd of spectators, munching on strawberries and cream, are questioning why I'm wearing a tennis skirt. But hey, at least they agree I have the legs for it.

Do you have control over whether you win this tennis match against me?

You can't answer "yes" to this, and you also can't answer "no". Even if you have a hitman sitting amongst the spectators, hired to take me out for humiliating you by wearing a tennis skirt, there is still the chance he will miss his target. Otherwise, you have some influence over the outcome of the match, but you can't control it completely. A tennis match could therefore be categorised as something over which we have some control.

Now you can divide this situation into the first two categories – things we can control and things that we can't control.

Sticking with the tennis match analogy, here are some examples of things you can control:

- Your training regime
- Your choice of coach
- The equipment you use
- The clothes you wear (it's harder to play tennis in a duffle coat)
- How much effort you put in
- How distracted you are by me wearing a tennis skirt

Note how all of these things fall into the categories of your thoughts and your actions. That being said, I could turn out to be a slightly hairier version of Pete Sampras. Despite you training hard, hiring the best coach, buying the best gear, playing harder than you ever have before AND refusing to be distracted by me wearing a tennis skirt . . . I could still annihilate you on the court.

That's because of a number of factors, including:

- My training regime
- My coach
- The equipment I've invested in
- The clothes I'm wearing (maybe the tennis skirt will give me the edge)
- How much effort I put in

All of these things, as well as my natural ability, are things that you simply can't control.

You can control your part in the tennis match; I can control my part of it. But neither of us has complete control of the tennis match or its outcome – we both have to just concentrate on those things we can control.

Analogy 2 – Racing a lift

This example came to me while I was on holiday with my partner and our two daughters. We had just enjoyed a day at the hotel pool and were heading back up to our room, from the ground level (floor 0) to our room on floor 4. My elder daughter, Sienna, suddenly declared that she wanted to race against the lift. My partner, Natalie, agreed to join her, while India and I took the lift. Thinking of Sienna's little legs and the speed of the lift, I was already looking forward to my triumphant victory (I can be a little over-competitive at times). Ready . . . steady . . . GO!

And what happened?

Just as I was about to press the button to go up to floor 4, someone at the basement level called the lift and we started going DOWN. A great start – we were even further from the finishing line. The lift door opened at the basement level, for someone who only wanted to travel up to floor 0. (How lazy is that? I was really starting to feel the pressure.) The lift stopped at the ground floor, our new lift companion got out . . . and someone else entered the lift. Nnggh! My heart sank as they pressed the button for the second floor – another delay to our journey.

By the time we reached floor 4, Sienna had mastered some of the world's most challenging sudoku puzzles and the Times crossword.

Again, looking at this situation, what did I have control of?

- Pressing the right button

- How quickly I pressed that button (definitely without letting India have a go)
- Whether I let other people get in the lift with us (in hindsight, maybe I should have been more ruthless)
- How quickly I pressed the other buttons when people got in the lift
- Whether I refused to let the newcomers choose the floors they wanted

What didn't I have control over?

- How fast Sienna and Natalie got to the fourth floor
- Other people using the lift to go up only one floor
- How quickly people got in the lift
- The speed of the lift

(And a few other things.)

I hope these two analogies have given you a good understanding of what you can and can't control in these two situations, which you should easily be able to translate to any other situation.

Your actions

Put simply, these are the things that you do. In the purest sense, no one else but us controls our actions. It could be argued that, for example, you are expected at work to behave a certain way and are told to do things. Even if you don't really want to do any of those things, you might feel you have to, as if you have no control. I would, however, argue that you always actually have a choice and control over everything you do. Even if you are certain you will jeopardise your position by not behaving a certain way or following orders, your actions are still ultimately up to you. For example, if you know you'd be fired if you finally cracked and threw a stapler at Barbara in Accounts Receivable because you're fed up of hearing her cocky progress reports every single hour – we all know a Barbara – your actions are still governed by you, according to your awareness of the consequences.

I feel it's essential here to mention abusive relationships. More often than not, victims of emotional or physical abuse feel in an inescapable situation in which they have little or no control. Without wanting to belittle such circumstances, I do still have to point out that we still *always* have control over our actions. In an abusive relationship, it is again the repercussions – the abuser's own actions – that will so often make the victim behave in a certain way. But the victim is then still choosing his or her own actions, usually in order to reduce the likelihood of further abuse.

If you're reading this and you are in an abusive relationship, please be aware that there are a number of organisations, run by experienced and sensitive people, founded specifically to help anyone suffering from abuse. At the time of writing, such organisations in the UK include the National Domestic Violence Helpline for women, freephone 0808 2000 247, and Men's Advice Line, freephone 0808 801 0327. Please speak out – one day you will thank yourself.

Let's get back now to your actions and how this chapter relates specifically to your wedding day.

What you as a couple control in terms of actions:

- Your selection of venue
- The types of supplier you use
- Which suppliers you choose
- What you and your partner wear
- How you arrange the format of your day
- Your food and drink choices
- Your choice of wedding theme
- How you organise the seating plan
- How much you spend
- Who you invite

I'm sure you're getting the idea now and will be able to add more to that list.

Most crucial is that the things that are often some of the most stressful things about wedding planning cannot be placed on that list, because they don't fall within your sphere of influence. Let's consider some of the biggest wedding stressors and think about them in terms of your own control.

I fully acknowledge that me saying "This isn't under your control" doesn't automatically make something any better or any easier. In the final three chapters, I will cover specific techniques on how to let go of even the most emotionally charged aspects of your life, once you have recognised them to be outside your sphere of influence. First, I only need to make you completely aware of how few factors you control in relation to your wedding.

By the end of this chapter, you will understand how that knowledge can be extremely beneficial to you and your potential stress levels.

A list of the top wedding stressors and your levels of control over them

Your bridesmaids liking their dresses

Typically, the style and colour of bridesmaids' dresses are chosen to fit in with the wedding theme and the bride's personal preferences, not to make the bridesmaids look frumpy.

In this respect, your control begins and ends with choosing the dress. You do not have control over the thoughts and feelings of your bridesmaids (or of anyone else, for that matter). If you are happy with your choice of dresses, it is then up to the bridesmaids to respect that choice, just as they would expect you to respect their choices for their weddings. By all means, listen to their concerns and try to find dresses that you think your bridesmaids will like. But remember always that their thoughts and feelings are not in your sphere of influence.

Guests not liking your choices

Your wedding day is about you and your partner coming together and celebrating your love, together with the people you love and respect the most. I personally feel that your wedding is the perfect opportunity for you and your partner to stamp your personalities onto a single day, to show everyone exactly who you are and what you cherish most.

This point, about guests potentially not liking your choices, is very similar to the previous one about the bridesmaids' dresses – you've made your choices for your wedding day for good reasons. You are not in control of other people's thoughts or feelings, meaning that they are outside your sphere of influence.

You've probably heard the quote "You can please some of the people all of the time, you can please all of the people some of the time, but you can't please all of the people all of the time". While I agree with that, I would take it one step further: if you try and please everyone, you'll end up pleasing no one.

Think of your guests and by all means arrange things at your wedding that you hope they will like, but please always remember that what they like is not under your control. And this is *your* day.

Family politics

It might well be that you have a fairy-tale family, where everyone gets along fine and no one has ever remarried (though, having said that, evil step-mothers are pretty standard to fairy tales too). Or it might well be that both of your sets of parents have suffered less than amiable divorces and haven't laid eyes on each other since. Plus, Cousin Joe fell out with Auntie Jane over something that happened five years ago, and they're both too stubborn to apologise.

No families are perfect but, while I've heard about some brides-to-be feeling worried about family politics in the run-up to their weddings, please rest assured that I have yet to notice uncomfortable situations on the day. Thankfully, people do manage to bury the hatchet, if only temporarily, for the sake of the happy couple. And above all, please always remember that any bad feeling between other people is most certainly out of your control. For your wedding day, however much people resolve to bury the hatchet depends entirely on their own thoughts and actions, and peace levels will depend in part on how much interaction certain people have with each other.

The only part of family politics in your control is the seating plan. Clearly, it is your responsibility to decide who sits with whom, but once you've separated Joe and Jane and anyone else who is likely to bicker, you're done. Whether all those people then do get on is not within your control.

The dreaded mother(-in-law) trying to take control

Mothers will almost always have envisaged how their son or daughter's wedding day will be and, depending on their own personality, they will sometimes try to exert some form of pressure, in order to make the day live up to their own expectations. If their designs conflict with your wedding plans, clearly this could be a source of anxiety or stress.

Let's look at the control here.

Do you have control over your mother(-in-law)'s personality?

No.

Do you have control over what your mother(-in-law) wants?

No.

Do you have control over her thoughts and actions?

No.

What do you have control over?

Your thoughts and your actions – nothing else.

Resisting the interference of a close family member can lead to a diplomatically challenging situation, especially if that person has strong opinions and an assertive personality. But it is paramount to your own tranquillity to always stay in touch with the fact that you can only control your thoughts and your actions.

If one of your mother(-in-law)'s suggestions is abhorrent to you and you can't imagine it being a part of your day at all, then it is simply down to you to use every ounce of diplomacy within yourself to control what you say and how you say it.

For example, simply let your mother know that you have no obligation to wear a pink bonnet down the aisle just as she and her mother, grandmother and great-grandmother did. If she doesn't like what you say or how you say it, then that once again is out of your control. As long as you feel you've been true to yourself and your wedding, you can be happy with what you've said and done – you can't control how your mother(-in-law) feels about it.

There's always the option of compromising on something that is not particularly important to you, or sacrificing one thing for the greater good of keeping her happy. But please always remember that you are NOT in control of any other person's thoughts or actions.

Seating plan

This is really simple – you have control over where people sit, and that's all.

It is very likely you already have a feeling of who is going to get on well together, and it's almost inevitable that you will want to spend some time working out how best to seat everyone. You've probably already heard stories about this part of wedding planning being a nightmare, but why not simply take control and decide to disprove that idea?

Get together with a few close friends or family members, lay on a load of nibbles and drinks, throw on some good music and hunker down to enjoy working through this conundrum. Write down the guests' names on separate pieces of paper, then have a laugh as you recount stories of who does/doesn't get on with whom and why. Keep shifting the pieces of paper around until you have found some way to keep arch enemies at opposite ends of the room and BFFs together.

If your seating-plan aides have any doubts about your preferences, that's fine – this is your wedding and your seating plan – you are in control, so the final choice is yours.

If it turns out on the day that someone doesn't like where they have been seated, you simply need to remember two things:

1. You're dealing with other people's thoughts and feelings, over which you have no control. This isn't your problem, especially if they can't be bothered to pretend they're having a nice time

AND

2. It's one bloody mealtime they have to get on for – you or your partner would be perfectly justified in telling them, "Suck it up, cupcake!"

Having to do it by yourself

A lot of brides feel that they're very much on their own when it comes to planning their big day and aren't getting enough support from partners, family members, bridesmaids, etc. That can, understandably, be an additional source of stress.

Remember (as if you could forget because I keep banging on about it) that you control ONLY your thoughts and your actions and nothing else.

Have you asked for help from people?

Have you let people know that you're finding it stressful?

People aren't mind readers (unless they're me) and, although your future partner *should* know that all this could become super-stressful and that planning a wedding can be very challenging, that doesn't mean that they actually *do* know.

Use what you're in control of to try and address the situation.

Tell people you're finding it hard.

Ask for help.

Ask for recommendations.

Assign jobs to people.

If you generally don't like asking other people for help, please change your thoughts and feelings – you're in control of those. It's not unusual to feel too proud to ask for help, or to hate feeling as if you're bothering people. But weddings have two very strong arguments for making you act differently: this will be one of the hardest things you've ever done – you'd have to be superhuman not to need some help. And weddings are exciting for everyone involved – anyone who cares about you will love to be given at least a small role and will thoroughly enjoy anything you ask them to do. It really is okay to ask for help.

If you do this and you still don't get help, then perhaps you need to be having a deeper discussion about the support you're receiving in your relationship and from friends and family. Still, though, you have to keep in mind that your own thoughts and actions are all that you control.

Facebook tagging and photos

Social media can be a blessing and a curse when it comes to your wedding day. Many people want their day to be kept exclusive to the select few who have been invited and want the photos of the day to be kept strictly to the professional ones that they've spent thousands on.

If you're one of these people and you don't want everyone to be constantly staring at their smartphones, with no risk of a crappy, blurry selfie of you and your drunk cousin on Instagram before you've even cut your cake, then I don't particularly blame you.

If you're planning a church wedding, it's pretty likely that the vicar will ask for all phones and cameras to be turned off during the ceremony. You might well demand the same if yours is a civil ceremony. This is an especially profound and personal time, when you and your partner will be exchanging emotionally charged life vows. Surely you'd prefer to feel that your guests are all with you in that moment, rather than poised glaring at their phones, trying to catch a killer shot? You've paid a photographer for that . . . and you only need to Google "wedding photos ruined by phones" to see why your photographer will be on your side in banning mobiles.

Please be aware that some people will think the phone ban won't apply to them, so don't be afraid of putting up a large sign, getting your MC or best man to make an announcement, and/or arranging a box at the door for guests to place their phones into as they arrive. Their phone isn't their pacemaker – being away from it for 30 minutes isn't going to be fatal – and it'll ensure that your guests are a lot more present and focused on your day.

However you decide to demand no phone pics, I'm afraid I'll have to remind you that this is where your control ceases. From there, it is down to people's respect for your wishes, which unfortunately is not within your control. If you realise later that some people still insisted on taking photos, you can only accept that there was nothing else you could do about it (and at least 97% of the guests listened).

Pressure to look great and how you look in photos

I think it's safe to say that every bride wants to look at her absolute best on her wedding day. Let's look at what is in your control here.

- The dress you choose
- Your diet – this will affect how much weight you gain or lose, as well as affecting the condition and appearance of your skin (or so make-up artist friends tell me)
- Whether you use a make-up artist
- Whether you use a hair stylist
- Any exercise regime you choose to do and your level of commitment

You don't control what your face looks like or your bone structure or your height. Genetics plays the biggest part in how you look, which is again not in your control.

There are three other aspects to all this, which override the discussion above about which parts of your appearance you can control:

1. Beauty is subjective – how many times have you and your friends disagreed over whether a certain celebrity is hot?

2. Beauty is nothing more than an opinion held by a person. That opinion is another person's thoughts, which you can't control. If anyone still doesn't think you're beautiful, after any changes you've made to the things you *can* control, then that's their issue, not yours

3. Attitude is as important as beauty. If you tell yourself and believe that you're a 10, then you will be a 10 – if you know that you look your best, it will shine out of you like a lighthouse on steroids. You might not be a 10 to everyone, but who cares – you are a 10 to the one you love

No matter which photographer you hire – the cheapest or the most expensive, the photography student or the top London wedding photographer – they will catch a few

CHAPTER 2 – UNDERSTANDING CONTROL

photos on the day of you looking, er, less than beautiful. Not because you are less than beautiful but because you will at some point be snapped mid-word or mid-yawn, or halfway through a raucous, less-than-attractive laugh. But here's the great news – you'll NEVER see these photos. Whereas the paparazzi will publish the worst possible photo of a celebrity leaving a nightclub at 2 am, your wedding photographer will only be trying to make you happy and showcase their skills. While creating the story of your day, they will take thousands of photos of you and pick only the very best of them to show you, which you will no doubt round down even further.

> SIDE NOTE: I cannot emphasise strongly enough the importance of spending wisely on your photographer. This isn't the same as hiring a plumber on someone's recommendation – you will have different taste from the newly wed friend who raves about her own photographer. Browse photos of a few photographers' previous weddings to find the types and style of photos that you like the best. However much you perfect your Stoic Bride approach, your wedding day will still be over all too quickly. But a talented photographer will capture the real feeling of the whole day, together with all the most important touches, so that you can remember it for ever, just how you want to remember it.

Bad weather

Bad weather is possibly a bride's worst nightmare. But seriously – you already know what I'm going to say about this – you have no control over the weather. I've performed in glorious sunshine at December weddings, I've performed in snowy weather in March and the worst wedding weather I've experienced was on a Saturday in July.

Brides plan, the weather laughs. All you can do is play the odds.

Let's get on to what you can control. Towards the end of Chapter 1, I said that, as a Stoic Bride, you will be prepared for failure and ready for success. And you certainly do have control over whether you build a contingency plan for the weather and how well you can put that plan together.

Here are some examples:

1. How would rain affect your day?
   Does it mean that your drinks reception would have to be moved inside? Are there outside areas not under cover that you and your guests wouldn't be able to avoid? If so, could you have umbrellas ready to hand out to everyone? Would these really need to be top-of-the-range white parasols, or would your guests be just as happy to choose from a colourful selection of borrowed umbrellas?

2. Where would you take your photos if the weather is terrible?
   Speak to your photographer about this – they will have faced this question any number of times and provided or experienced a range of different solutions. Here's some reassurance: I've seen some absolutely stunning and unusual wedding photos that have *taken advantage* of rainy conditions.

3. What else can you do to prepare yourself and your wedding day as much as possible for the worst-case weather scenario?
   Walk yourself through the different parts of your day, imagining how you and your guests would be affected by rain, and think of any possible solutions. You will then have done all that is under your control.

If it does rain, you can either be annoyed or you can choose to embrace it. If you get annoyed, the weather isn't going to change – you'll only be in the same situation but feeling stressed. If you embrace the rain and put your contingency plans into place, you'll feel prepared and be able to live happily in the moment.

Comparison with other weddings

The more competitive people out there will long for their wedding day to be the best wedding that their guests have ever been to. Fair enough, if you're dropping tens of thousands of pounds on a single day, it's understandable that you're going to want it to be extra-special.

Comparing ourselves with others is, to a certain extent, part of human nature. But Stoic philosophy will give you ways to counter the negative effects, bringing together the two pillars of Stoicism that we have mentioned so far – gratitude and control. In terms of gratitude, you should already be strongly considering how grateful you are that you are in a position to bring everyone together, book all of your wedding suppliers, host your wedding in a tremendous location, etc. Making an unfavourable comparison of your wedding with someone else's goes against the grain in terms of gratitude.

This relates to a quote from Epicurus: "Do not spoil what you have by desiring what you have not. What you have now was once among that which you desired."

Do you really want to allow yourself to get into the mood or mindset where on the day you're comparing your own wedding with others or wondering whether other people are making that comparison? The only thing that will achieve is spoiling your day for yourself by making you feel discontented, while not being fully present and living in the moment.

The wedding you have organised is definitely a thing that "you once desired". Now that you're actually experiencing, it, don't spoil the wedding for yourself by thinking about someone else's.

In terms of control, it always comes back to the same thing – comparisons that any of your guests make are *their* thoughts. As you well know by now, you are not in control of their thoughts or feelings.

All you are in control of is the wedding that you create; if you've created a wedding that you are happy with, that is all you can do.

Bored guests

There's no doubt that you want your guests to have an enjoyable time at your wedding and remember it for the right reasons. The prospect of guests being bored is to brides as kryptonite is to Superman.

There are three main times at a wedding with a traditional format where guests are most likely to experience boredom:

1. Between the end of the ceremony and the start of the wedding breakfast
2. During the photos
3. Between the end of the wedding breakfast and the start of the evening reception

These are typically long periods where there's not a lot going on, other than standing around waiting for the next part of the day, when your guests might well be feeling hungry and fed up, making small talk and watching the clock.

Now, whilst you're not in control of your guests' thoughts and feelings, you are in control of planning ahead to avoid boring situations. Organising entertainment, garden games, treasure hunts, quizzes and photo booths are just a few of the plethora of boredom-busting options.

In my experience of performing at hundreds of weddings, they provide sure-fire ways of turning the quieter times of the day into some of the most memorable ones.

Whilst you still can't 100% guarantee guests won't be bored, you'll be swinging the odds massively in your favour if you organise some entertainment. Remember, though, that providing entertainment is all you control. You might still be unlucky with a few guests who'd rather not be watching the magician being completely awesome – there's just no pleasing some people!

Picky eaters

Your control starts and stops at choosing the food.

If people have dietary requirements, then of course you have to cater for them. Then there will be a certain number of people who are simply naturally picky eaters. You have no control over that, and it is extremely unlikely you will ever find a meal that suits everyone.

If you know that your family or friends have very different tastes and preferences, and you know you will feel uncomfortable watching people not eating, you could opt for a varied buffet. If one person still feels they can only eat the breadsticks, they will simply have to eat lots of them and start planning their next meal at home.

If you are lucky enough to have mostly adventurous eaters amongst your guests, why not look for an audaciously unusual meal? Giving people new taste experiences is a great way to add a layer of unforgettability (this is not a word) to your day.

Whatever you choose, just keep in mind that you cannot control other people's tastes and you can't please everyone, so you simply don't need to feel stressed about this.

The best man's speech

Is the best man at your wedding an utter douchebag? Would you really prefer it was someone else? Unfortunately, this is likely to be an action and choice that is made by your partner, giving you no control over that choice. You can by all means voice your opinion, but this is all you can do.

Often one of the funniest and most heart-warming parts of the day is the best man's speech. Your partner is almost inevitably going to get a good ribbing and there are likely to be some slightly unsavoury stories told, which will get everyone in the room laughing.

Once again, you have no control at all over this. The most you can do is to suggest some guidelines of what's appropriate – your great-grandmother probably really doesn't need to hear the story about how your partner necked a bottle of whisky on his stag do and then threw up all over a stripper in Vegas. However, providing guidelines gives zero guarantee of them actually being followed – what the best man says is out of your control.

If the best man does say something that upsets you, remind yourself again that this was never in your control – it is your response to this external event which will determine whether your tranquillity is affected.

Let's have a proper think about this – everyone at your wedding is close to you and backing you all the way. If the best man says something to embarrass you and your partner, your guests will recognise how uncomfortable you might be feeling and feel critical only of the best man for what he has said, not of you or your partner. Any protective feelings of love towards you will thereby only be amplified, and everyone will feel nothing but admiration for you if you laugh it off and move on. You can control your actions, and your feelings will be improved if you force yourself to get over it (which will be easier after you have mentally prepared yourself by reading this chapter).If you hadn't known anything about the stripper in Vegas, you can also control your feelings about that unfortunate revelation. Neither you nor your partner has any control over the past and it is a fact of life that people

CHAPTER 2 – UNDERSTANDING CONTROL

make mistakes; for the sake of your wedding day, it will only help you to enjoy your day more if you can decide to ignore any feelings of hurt.

That doesn't mean to say that you should put up with any hurtful actions from your partner, though! I'll talk to you more about this in the final three chapters, but in short for now: practising Stoic philosophy doesn't mean that all of a sudden you're immune from upset. You will still always be human and as such you're allowed to get upset.

> SIDE NOTE: This last section, about the best man's speech, has been particularly difficult to write without sounding sexist and homophobic. Regardless of your gender or sexuality, please simply mould everything I say to your own situation, to save me having to write "his/her", "best man/woman" (and so on) a thousand times in this book. I am over the moon that same-sex marriage is (at long last) openly accepted, and women are of course now generally accepted in any role in life, including at weddings. Regardless of whether you are a male or a female organising a wedding (for your male or female partner), and whether you have a best man or a best woman, a host of "best people", or if you have done away with speeches altogether, I hope you will accept that every single principle in this book happily applies to any gender, any sexuality, any wedding and to life in general.

Accepting the limitations of control

The bottom line with regards to Stoicism and control is that, as soon as you have recognised that you have zero control over something, it must instantly be disregarded as a source of stress and anxiety, and must not be allowed to affect your tranquillity.

Easier said than done though, right?

Yes, you're right.

Recognising what you can control and disregarding things outside your control are skills, which, like any other skill, need to be learnt. Once learnt, skills can then be honed by repetition and practice.

There are a few exercises, which are pretty similar yet distinct, which will help you learn this skill and then hone it further. The second of these exercises will be of particular use to you if you often find yourself unable to get to sleep at night, due to things you're worrying about, which are even more likely if you're feeling stressed about something like a wedding. The third exercise below is arguably even more useful than the first two.

**EXERCISE 3
SEGMENTATION**

This is a really simple practice and should be done EVERY time any source of anxiety or stress tries to disrupt your tranquillity. Potentially the only difficult part is remembering to do it every time anxiety or stress presents itself.

Here are the steps you need to take:

1. Define the source of the anxiety, e.g. "The florist has told me that there's a worldwide petunia shortage and they will now be 100 times more expensive"

2. Define whether this is

    a. Something you can control
    b. Something you can't control
    c. Something you have some control over

3. If a.: use whatever thoughts or actions you can to resolve the situation
   If b.: state clearly to yourself that you do not have any control over it. You can even do this out loud to yourself in a mirror to make it sink in further
   If c.: recognise the part of the situation that you can control and see "If a." above; for the remainder of the situation, see "If b."

That's it – you're done.

If you have any doubts about how this could ever be effective, please sit back and think very carefully about the following question. Is there ANY benefit to you at all in getting upset, angry and losing your tranquillity over something that you can do absolutely nothing about?

As I mentioned earlier, in the final three chapters I will clarify that you ARE allowed to be upset when bad things happen. But for now, the only relevant point is that getting upset about something you can't control will get you nowhere.

The best example of this in practice

Have you ever been driving, when you're running late and having to do your make-up in the car (I know I have), and then you get stuck for ages behind another driver? They're driving a grey Fiat Cinquecento and from behind they look as if they're at least 125 years old. They're struggling to see over the steering wheel and they're driving at 16 mph in a 40 mph zone.

There's a constant stream of traffic from the other direction, removing any possibility of you overtaking. You're begging the other driver from the deepest part of your soul to follow a different route from yours, but at every roundabout they keep selecting the exit you need to take.

What control do you have of this situation in terms of what you can make the other driver do?

Clearly, causing the maddeningly slow driver to fishtail is an option, as is sideswiping them off the road, but neither of those options bears reasonable consideration, especially if you don't want to be in jail on your wedding day. Slightly more legal (but nevertheless ineffective) options

CHAPTER 2 – UNDERSTANDING CONTROL

include tailgating them, beeping furiously or using any combination of expletives that you know.

We already know that we are not in control of anyone else's thoughts or actions. Your real options in this situation boil down to just two outcomes:

1. To arrive late, turning up flustered and angry, with a hoarse voice from screaming at the other driver for the entire duration of the trip

OR

2. Realising that you have no control over this situation and resolving yourself to being late but turning up calm, having used the extra time to prepare yourself mentally for whatever you're about to be late for

> SIDE NOTE: You were in control of what time you left the house. So why intimidate a pensioner by beeping because of your mistake – imagine if someone was doing that to your Granny!

Whichever of the two options above you choose, you will be late, and your anger will not improve anything at all.

I'm sure this driving situation is easy enough to understand. You see you have no control and thus you can then choose to stay calm, right?

Is it actually much of a stretch of the imagination for you to mentally replace that driving situation with one where a bridesmaid doesn't like her dress, or someone doesn't like their food, or any other possible stressors at your wedding?

I really don't think that it is.

It is the ability to quickly recognise the level or control you have in any situation and how to respond accordingly that will be vital to you attaining and keeping your tranquillity and becoming a Stoic Bride.

EXERCISE 4
SLEEP BASKETS

Insomniacs and worriers – this one is especially for you. It's an exercise that, during my time as a hypnotherapist, I recommended people did before going to sleep at night. It might feel like a lot to read through and remember, but after a couple of practices you will realise how easy and enjoyable the exercise is.

You might be happy to keep your eyes closed, as suggested below, for this exercise. However, please don't feel you have to if that is difficult or uncomfortable in any way – you will still gain from the exercise if you follow it with your eyes open.

If you are happy to shut your eyes, you can simply read through the whole exercise a couple of times before starting, to memorise the steps (don't worry – the steps are logical and easy to remember). Or, if or when you are somewhere you can listen in peace to an audio recording, go to www.chrispiercymagic.co.uk/bwp-exercises to hear my extended explanation and recording of this exercise, which will be even easier to follow and more effective.

1. Get into bed and make yourself comfortable
2. If your partner is in bed with you, simply make them aware that you're going to sleep and don't want to be disturbed
3. Close your eyes, then begin to imagine yourself in the most relaxing, happy place you can think of
   - Imagine what your place looks like, taking time to look at some of the things there
   - Imagine what sounds you would hear, e.g. the sound of sea waves
   - Imagine feelings you would experience, e.g. the warmth of the sun
   - Imagine any smells there might be, e.g. the aroma of the ocean
   - Imagine any tastes you might experience, e.g. the refreshing beer you've been drinking

   You can of course adapt this exercise to any place or situation where you feel most relaxed. If you love Christmas time at home, for example, you could imagine the sound of the log fire, the feeling of sitting in your favourite armchair, the smell of Christmas dinner and the taste of mince pies. Most importantly, allow yourself to engage fully with all of your senses, really picturing yourself in your place and imagining all the related sensations as if you were really there. It will become such a beautiful place within your mind, it feels almost real

4. Now you're imagining yourself here in this wonderful place, turn your attention to any thoughts in your mind that are bothering you. Acknowledge that they are JUST thoughts – they don't actually mean anything. You're not there to judge the thoughts but only to be aware of them. I recommend you start off with only two or three thoughts, until you get used to the remaining steps below

5. Imagine now that there are three baskets in front of you, which represent the trichotomy of control: one basket with the label "can control", one with "can't control" and one with "some control". Now imagine that you are able to take one of the thoughts you've noticed from inside your head and examine it, then decide which basket it belongs in. Then simply put the thought into that basket and then move onto another thought. Repeat this until you have no new thoughts to imagine

6. Now go back to the thoughts in the "some control basket". Take them out of the basket and re-examine them. Imagine splitting each "some control"

thought into two parts – the part you control and the part you don't control – then put those newly divided parts into the appropriate baskets

7. I'd like you now to think of the best way, in your mind, to destroy all the thoughts over which you have no control. Are you going to set fire to them? Soak them in acid? Throw them in the air and watch them blow away in the wind? Simply choose the way that symbolises most clearly to you those thoughts being truly removed from your mind, then imagine destroying all the other "can't control" thoughts in the same way. You have no control over them, so there is no point at all holding onto them

8. You are now left only with the thoughts that you can control. Pick them up and examine them one by one. With each thought, ask yourself "What can I do about this right now?" If the answer is nothing, then destroy the thought exactly as you did in the previous step. Repeat until you're left with the thoughts over which you have control and are able to take action to resolve right now (if any)

9. If you can take action to resolve any remaining thoughts that are bothering you, do that now

10. Scan your brain for any residual sources of anxiety or thoughts and repeat steps 7) to 9) until there are no thoughts left. Then, with your brain completely clear, let yourself drift off to sleep. If you're doing

this exercise during the day, slowly allow your mind to reconnect with your surroundings and, whenever you're ready, open your eyes and continue your day. You will feel significantly more relaxed, and stronger in dealing with the day ahead

EXERCISE 5
ACCURATE GOAL SETTING

This exercise goes one step further, removing the need for you even to think about having to eliminate the things you can't control.

Sound good? I think so!

This is all about the goals you're going to be setting yourself in relation to your wedding day itself. Your goals can be split into two different categories: external goals and internal goals.

External goals are ones for which you have no, or only some, control over the outcome. For some control, an example would be "I want to compile my wedding guest list without causing any upset". For no control, an example would be "I want everyone to think my wedding was the best wedding they've ever been to".

Internal goals are ones over which only you have control, for example "I want to drop a dress size before my wedding day" or "I want to create a wedding day that I am happy with". There's not necessarily anything that will

CHAPTER 2 – UNDERSTANDING CONTROL

prevent your external and internal goals being achievable. However, I'm sure you can already see how much easier and less frustrating it will be to focus primarily on achieving your internal goals, the ones you can control.

You might well, in theory, be able to create a wedding that everyone thinks is the best wedding they've ever been to. But, with the levels of control you have over everything needed for that, the amount of stress involved and the lack of tranquillity you will almost certainly experience, there is of course a high chance that your wedding planning will become an unenjoyable experience for you. It's worth considering whether you would wish that on any bride-to-be, and why then you should deserve it.

Now let's look at an internal goal: "I want to create a wedding day that I am happy with". I am sure you can already sense just how much easier that goal will be to achieve. The very fact that you are already reframing your own expectations, and your feelings of gratitude for all the good things, will make the "happy" part of that goal incredibly less challenging.

Sure, there will still be some ups and downs, but hey – there's got to be some excitement attached to making decisions and finding solutions. As long as you fully appreciate that you only need to think about your own thoughts and feelings, the things you can control, you will only need to think about your own preferences while considering what is important to you about your wedding. So, from now on, please only set yourself INTERNAL goals!

Conclusion on understanding control

After reading this chapter and practising for just a short time, I am confident that you will find it easy to recognise the level of control you have over any aspect of your life.

It might take you a little longer to fully develop the mindset of putting anything you can't control out of your mind and banning any associated negative emotions, but that's okay – you will get there. After a life of being bombarded with endless pressures around things we can't control, it's natural that it can be harder to learn to ignore them. I have, though, aimed to cover all the typical wedding stressors here, explaining why and how you can simply let go of any stress and frustration related to them, to give you a great start in your own wedding planning.

There will be readers thinking I've missed something vital. "What about compiling the guest list?" "I'm stuck on even choosing the theme." "Budgeting is by far the hardest bit!"

Please believe that I'm not now feeling smug when I say, "That's out of my control". But, in the same way that you, say, can't please everyone with your seating plan, I of course can't predict what is most stressful to you

CHAPTER 2 – UNDERSTANDING CONTROL

about planning your wedding. If I've missed the one most important stressor for you, you only need to go through the simple steps of determining your level of control, acting only on parts you can control, and deciding not to feel stressed about the rest.

> "What really frightens and dismays us is not external events themselves, but the way in which we think about them. It is not things that disturb us, but our interpretation of their significance."
>
> Epictetus

Stoic thinking around control is fundamental to your journey to becoming a Stoic Bride. Being able to let go of anything you can't control is one of the most important life lessons and skills that any person can learn, bride or not. Once you get used to thinking about everything in this way, you'll be a big step further towards Stoic tranquillity and you'll have a lot more time for things that are truly important.

Being a Stoic Bride will empower you to:

- Understand your sphere of influence
- Focus on anything you can control
- Accept and not worry about what you can't control
- Set yourself only internal goals

CHAPTER 3
Wanting and needing

You have everything you need.

That might sound like just another of my bold statements, but if you consider the definition of "need", it won't seem quite as bold.

Need, verb: require a thing because it is necessary and indispensable.

What do you actually *need* for your wedding? Before we try to answer that, let's delve deeper into a more pertinent question: what do you actually need in your life?

Human needs

American psychologist Abraham Maslow created a "Hierarchy of Human Needs", which provided a full breakdown of what human beings require within their lives in order to attain happiness. I'm going to cover this only briefly – enough to give you a clear understanding; there's a great full explanation on Wikipedia if this really interests you.

Maslow's Hierarchy of Human Needs is usually portrayed as a segmented pyramid. As with a physical pyramid, the bottom layer has to be secure before the next layer can be worked on or attained.

The layers in Maslow's pyramid, from bottom to top:

- Physiological needs
- Safety
- Love/belonging
- Esteem
- Self-actualisation

Physiological needs

This starts with the minimum physical requirements that a human actually needs to survive. Without these quite firmly in place, the other pyramid levels cannot even be considered:

- Oxygen
- Water
- Food
- Sleep

- Clothing (as basic protection – not designerwear)
- Shelter
- Sex

These are actually the only things a human needs to survive (you may question the inclusion of the last entry on the list – this isn't my list, so don't shoot the messenger!). You might also be thinking that you need everything above this bottom level, such as feeling safe and loved, but those don't determine whether a human being lives or dies. Anything beyond your physiological needs reflects the achievement of happiness or contentment – the more of these needs that are met, the more content a human feels.

You might be reading this thinking, "Hang on, Chris – you already did a chapter on gratitude. I understand that I need to be grateful for oxygen, food, sleep, etc". There is a crossover with gratitude and you will gain from feeling grateful for these things, but that's not the route we're going down in this chapter.

Piercy's Wedding Hierarchy

Let's apply the same principle of needs to your wedding, giving us a pyramid of wedding needs. What would define the very base of the pyramid, without which the wedding wouldn't exist? What would come at the very tip of the pyramid, without which the wedding would still work absolutely fine – there would be something missing, but the wedding would be far from a disaster?

This would give us what I call the Piercy's Wedding Hierarchy.

Level 0 – Base level

- Two people who want to marry each other or enter into a civil partnership/union
- Someone qualified to conduct the ceremony to make the marriage/union official
- Somewhere licensed to conduct the ceremony
- Two witnesses

And that's it.

Level 1 – Who and where

- A venue for the reception
- Wedding guests

Level 2 – Basic guest needs

- Food
- Drink
- Toilets

Level 3 – Experience for the bride(s) and/or groom(s)

- Rings

CHAPTER 3 – WANTING AND NEEDING

- Wedding dress(es) and/or suit(s)
- Wedding outfits for the bridesmaids/ushers/best man
- Photographer and/or videographer
- Make-up artist
- Hair stylist

Level 4 – Experience for the guests

- Entertainment
- Music
- Wedding theme, venue styling

Level 5 – Finishing touches

- Wedding cake
- Flowers
- Invitations and other wedding stationery
- Table decorations and wedding favours
- Special lighting
- Wedding website
- Wedding cars
- Live band
- Fireworks

- Gifts for mothers, bridesmaids, ushers, etc
- Guest book

I'll stop there – there are hundreds of optional extras, which brides-to-be might choose in order to make their weddings special, quirky or entertaining. There wouldn't be room on the pyramid to list them all.

Here's the most important part of this whole chapter: everything after level 0 is open to interpretation. My list and its order of importance reflect my own interpretation of a wedding day; other people might give an entirely different order of hierarchy. Someone who runs a wedding-stationery business, for example, might consider their products of level 4 importance and see entertainment as a level 5 finishing touch.

All of this is subjective . . . apart from level 0. You need everything at level 0 in order to get married. You don't *need* anything else for a wedding to take place.

Of course, unless you're eloping to Gretna Green to marry in absolute privacy and seclusion, you will also need the items in level 1 and, by proxy, level 2 as well.

Prioritising for your big day

Let's look now at the remaining levels. All the items in levels 3, 4 and 5 are things you might very much desire, but they're not things that you *need* – your wedding will still be a wedding without them. I would, however, postulate that not having *any* of the things in those levels might well lead to your day feeling dull and forgettable . . . or worse still, unforgettable for all the wrong reasons.

The only important thing for you is identifying what is really important to you and your partner. And I have devised a simple series of questions to help you to prioritise for your big day.

Working out what is most important to you

Imagine that it's the day after your wedding and everything went *exactly* as planned – you now feel nothing but glowing happiness about the day on which you betrothed your love for your now spouse. Now consider these four questions:

1. What is the most important thing you'd like to be thinking, retrospectively, about your wedding?

2. What is the obstacle most likely prevent your answer to question 1 from happening?

3. What is your plan to achieve your answer to question 1?

4. What steps are you taking to overcome your answer to question 2?

You may have a few answers to question 1. If so, go through the other three questions for each answer.

Here's an example answer to ensure understanding.

Example answers

1. What is the most important thing you'd like to be thinking, retrospectively, about your wedding?
That everything ran smoothly and everyone had a great time

This would then be split into two separate answers:

- That everything ran smoothly
- That everyone had a good time

Now we answer the next two questions for these answers, firstly "That everything ran smoothly":

2. What is the biggest obstacle most likely to prevent everything running smoothly?
    - Everything being done by the right people at the right time
    - All suppliers doing what they've been instructed to do
3. What is your plan to achieve these?
    - Write clear details for friends and family who are helping; ensure that the venue's wedding coordinator knows the plan for the day
    - Carefully select professional wedding suppliers, especially for those most important things

CHAPTER 3 – WANTING AND NEEDING

- Ensure that contracts are signed with every supplier and, in the weeks leading up to the wedding, confirm what each supplier needs to do and when
- Make sure that all suppliers have the number of someone at the venue they can contact in the case of an emergency

Only one example, but it's an absolutely solid one. Thinking back to what we control again for a second – is there really much more than can be done than that? I think it is more or less all you can do to ensure that everything runs smoothly.

And now back to the second answer, "That everyone had a good time":

1. What is the obstacle most likely to prevent everyone from having a good time?
   - A lot of my guests not knowing each other and not having anything in common
   - Waiting around for photos and during the room turnaround
2. What is your plan to ensure that your guests are having a good time and what's your plan for the quieter times of the day?
   - Make sure there's a good amount of free alcohol and canapés to stop people getting hangry
   - Arrange entertainment for the drinks reception, during photos and the bit after the meal to

provide some talking points and keep people occupied
- Book a wedding magician;* does anyone know a good one?

Again, one example answer but with a (*very) solid answer.

This isn't as much an exercise as good, straightforward questions to ask yourself in order to identify what is important on your day from your own perspective. Different people's answers will vary massively, but your specific responses will be key to determining what you need to focus your efforts on, in order to find yourself in that blissful state at the start of this section, where you were imagining it being the day after your wedding and that everything went exactly as planned.

Your guests' experience

Again, please imagine that it is the day after your wedding and everything went *exactly* as planned. You'll notice that the focus of this section is on your guests' experience; while we know by now that you can't control other people's thoughts and feelings, I can't imagine many brides-to-be thinking only about themselves, without aiming to provide an enjoyable experience for everyone (which, in turn, can make the day more enjoyable for the bride). The only important thing you need to bear in mind again here is that you can't please everyone – please focus only on *generally* providing a good experience for *most* of your guests when you're thinking about the following questions and answers.

1. What is the most important thing you'd want your guests to be saying about your day in terms of their experience of your wedding?
2. What's the obstacle most likely to prevent this from happening?
3. What is your plan to achieve your answer to question 1?
4. What steps are you taking to overcome your answer to question 2?

I don't think another example is required here – simply work through the questions and you will gain insight into how you will be able feel tranquil and confident about your guests' experience of the day.

The purpose of these two Q&A tasks was to begin to prioritise which of the things from levels 3, 4 and 5 in the wedding-hierarchy pyramid you need to focus on most or, arguably, the things around which you need to structure your budget.

Rolexes and Ferraris

It's Saturday early evening, your mum suddenly offers to babysit and, by pure coincidence, you hear from some old school friends. They're back in town for the night and are suggesting a fantastic night out, starting at the swanky new restaurant and ending up at your favourite nightclub.

What luck? But a sudden realisation washes over you and you rush to your bedroom, turn on the light and fling open your wardrobe. Falling to your knees like Willem Dafoe in Platoon, you look to the heavens, screaming,

"NOOOOOOOOOOOOOOOOOOOOOOOOOOO!"

Tears begin to well as you open your eyes and gaze desperately into the wardrobe. Staring hostilely back at you are six pairs of jeans, eight strappy tops, seven non-strappy tops, four pairs of jeggings, three jumper dresses, three maxi dresses, six slouchy jumpers, four out-out dresses, eight t-shirts, five pairs of shorts, four coats and 38 pairs of shoes . . . you have NOTHING to wear tonight. You're somehow going to have to make it to the shops for an outfit before you go out tonight, and it's already 4 pm.

Okay, I'll now remove my tongue from my cheek and try not to feel the thousands of daggers being shot my way.

When we get the chance to go out, we can feel a certain social pressure to look fashionable, not to be wearing something everyone's seen, and to look scorchingly hot. Nine times out of ten, the clothes we already have just don't seem to fit the bill. But this is all down to perspective.

Let's say you weren't meeting up with old friends, it wasn't your first night out in a decade, and you were only going to the shops to buy some milk. In those circumstances, the only requirement in terms of clothing would be that you are clothed, unless you happened to be a radical naturist not afraid of being arrested for parading naked around a supermarket. For most of us, it would be perfectly acceptable to pop to the shops wearing a hoodie and some faded jogging bottoms.

However, faced with the prospect of a swanky night on the town, although you would feel physically comfortable (and legal) in your jogging bottoms and hoodie combo, the altered circumstances dictate different clothing requirements. In order for you to feel emotionally confident and satisfied with the image you are projecting, you feel you 100% need to wear something different from the clothes currently in your wardrobe.

Let's take this example in a slightly different direction.

You find yourself in the middle of the Sahara Desert and all you can see is sand, sand and more sand. And a scorching hot sun. It's pushing 50°C, you drank the last of your water over an hour ago, and your only option is to continue walking.

Another 30 minutes pass, then you suddenly spot the outline of a figure in the distance – a man, who appears to be walking towards you. With your feet and body aching and your mouth so dry with thirst it's beginning to hurt, you muster all your strength to reach the man as quickly as possible.

You can't believe your luck – when you reach the man, you find out that he is a salesman. Not only that, but you haven't lost your purse.

"Water, waterrrrrrrrrrrr . . ." you rasp at the salesman.

"You look exhausted, madam. Would you like to buy this Tiffany necklace? Its recommended retail price is over £3,000, but it's yours today for only £20."

While you know that you have exactly £20 in your purse, your answer is obvious: "Nooo [dry cough], I just want water."

"Pffffft, I can't help you there, I'm afraid", and the man trudges off.

A little while later, your life slowly seeping from your body, you see another person ahead. He's dressed the same as the last man – it must be another salesman!

You try to say "Water!", but it sounds more like "Wassup!" from the 90s Budweiser adverts.

"Good afternoon, madam. Would you like to buy the Mona Lisa?"

"The original Mona Lisa?" you manage.

"Yes, it's priceless. It would fetch well over £50 million at auction but I'm bored of carrying it, so it's yours for only £20."

CHAPTER 3 – WANTING AND NEEDING

The thought very briefly crosses your mind how amazing it is that, while nearly perishing in the Sahara Desert, you've managed to find not one but two salesman who seem to speak perfect English.

Your mind quickly returns to the even more astonishing fact that you are being offered one of the world's most expensive paintings for next to nothing. But that feels immaterial now – all you need is water, so you politely decline the painting.

Suddenly, you spot see a third salesman.

"Water!" he says, the single word summarising his robust business model – selling water in the desert is about as easy as it gets.

"Yes, yes – I'll take it all – I don't care how much it is. Just give it to me, please!" you exclaim, your voice sounding like you've been gargling gravel for the last week.

"£10 for a litre bottle," he says, with a warm smile.

"I'll take two," you say. "Actually, I'll take it all and pay you anything that you want for the rest once I make it out of here."

He gives you all of his water and a small umbrella to keep the sun off, and you miraculously make it out of the desert. Upon returning home, you send the salesman £1,000 for his 10 bottles of water and the small umbrella. It was the best deal of your entire life.

This is, of course, a story about value, and how value shifts massively, depending on circumstances as well as personal perception and preferences.

But what does this have to do with your wedding? Don't worry, I'm getting there.

Finally talking about Rolexes and Ferraris

Why do people buy a Rolex? Why do people buy a Ferrari? They don't buy them only because they need a watch or need a car. They definitely don't feel they need them just to tell the time or to get from point A to B.

We live our lives through the stories that we tell ourselves. You'll find a full chapter on storytelling in Chapter 8; for now, this is about how storytelling relates to status. It's not at all unusual for people to tell themselves stories about how they feel their (apparent or relative) success should be made known to others, alongside reminding themselves of it too.

This means that, although a £7.99 Casio Illuminator can tell the time just as well as a £10,000 Rolex, for them it just doesn't cut it.

I don't want you to think that I'm hating on high-end products or saying that they're pointless. The reason I've chosen watches and cars as examples is so that I can draw on my own experiences and share them with you.

CHAPTER 3 – WANTING AND NEEDING

My aim here is, essentially, to illustrate perspective; I'll get around to weddings in a minute.

I am not a car person at all. That's just me. There are certain cars I think look awesome, but I have absolutely no desire to spend my hard-earned money on a Maserati. I have one goal and one goal only: reliability. Hence, at the time of writing, I am currently driving an 11-year-old Toyota Yaris, given to me by my uncle when he bought a new car. My Toyota has done less than 30,000 miles, I haven't had a single problem with it (ever), and it gets me happily from point A to point B, occasionally via point C.

Would I turn down a brand-new Audi if it was offered to me? Absolutely not.

Would anything change if I did have a new Audi? Internally – definitely not. Externally – I would hope not too (remembering, of course, that we can't control the external anyway).

The reason I mentioned the £7.99 Casio Illuminator was because I actually used to wear one. A few years later, I upgraded to a Casio A168WA-1YES, bought for around £30. This was because I felt my old Illuminator was beginning to look a little childish, especially as I was beginning to work at higher-end weddings amongst people with money.

For Christmas 2017 my partner, Natalie, very generously bought me a new Michael Kors watch which, with the greatest respect to Casio, blew my old watch out of the water. Wearing it, I felt like I had upgraded not just the watch but myself too, in some small way. The new watch felt right, and worked so much better with all my suits, my brand and my working environment. It was also given to me at a very meaningful time (pun intended).

Perhaps if there were a lot of people who saw me arriving at events, then the type of car I drive would have more value to me. But people rarely see me arrive or leave, so having a great car doesn't really have any value to me at all.

Now, what are the stories you're telling yourself about your wedding day?

The importance of value

I'm going to come straight out and tell you that I really don't see any point in spending money or time on buttonholes, i.e. the flowers that go in the lapel buttonholes of the men's suits. This genuinely isn't me telling you that you shouldn't value those floral embellishments, but here's my explanation for why they don't carry value for me.

I understand that the buttonholes are designed to be on theme with the other flowers, including the bride's bouquet, but I would rather have the money for them in my pocket. The same could even be said for all the flowers at a wedding. I don't dislike flowers; in fact, I do like buying my partner flowers and I've also had the privilege of seeing some utterly stunning flower arrangements and centrepieces. But, in terms of a wedding, they're just not for me. Nearly everything at a wedding barely lasts a day – note: I am NOT talking about the marriage here – therefore, the flowers simply don't add sufficient value to me to justify their cost. Going back to the desert analogy, buttonholes and maybe even all the flower arrangements are the equivalent of me being offered the Tiffany necklace for £20 when what I actually need is water.

In contrast, if I were organising your wedding, I would consider the photographer to be one of the most important things. The photographer is going to capture memories of your day, which will last for years and years – arguably for ever. I therefore place a very high value on the choice of photographer and would allocate it considerably more attention and budget than the flowers.

Now, it might well be that you have a love bordering on obsession for flowers. Perhaps the smell and atmosphere created by all the floral designs epitomise for you the whole meaning of love at your wedding. Perhaps the men's suits simply wouldn't look complete to you without the accompanying buttonhole. Or it might be that you are looking forward to creating the bouquets and other floral arrangements from your own garden flowers, which will cost pennies but make a memorable statement in those everlasting photographs of your day.

My own take on flowers is my own personal perspective – nothing more. My sole reason for telling you about that perspective is to help you to start reframing anything and everything you consider for your wedding. If you feel that you "have" to have flowers because, er, that's what everyone has at their wedding, please don't hesitate to challenge that perception. After all, some of the most memorable weddings you have attended (or will ever attend) were (or will be) made all the more memorable because the bride and groom did everything *their* way.

As you run through your list of everything you need for your wedding, please question the real value of every single item, including how much money you will have to spend on something that will no longer exist after your wedding day. I'm not saying this to be morbid or to make you feel bad about anything you truly value. This is only to help you to ground yourself in reality as a Stoic Bride.

Cost actually isn't that important

Read that subheading again.

I'm not even joking – cost isn't really that important at all.

"But Chris, we're on a really tight budget and have to watch every penny we're spending!" If you are saying that, then you're actually proving my point even further, believe it or not. Let me explain.

CHAPTER 3 – WANTING AND NEEDING

When it comes to products and services, there are two distinct things that affect a purchasing decision:

How much does it cost?

What is its value?

Imagine you have a terminal illness (not a very cheery opener – stick with me). You're fading away and you're about to lose everything you have. Someone tells you that they have the power to cure your illness and allow you to live a full life, but you have to give them everything you own. You'll be left with only your friends, your family and the clothes that you're wearing.

Would you take that deal? Who wouldn't?

The cost of the deal is potentially hundreds of thousands of pounds, but the value? You simply can't put a price on it. Value can't really be thought of in terms of money. Value is what something means to you, what something does for you, and what it prevents from happening – it's more about experience than about monetary cost. This is why cost isn't actually that important at all. In terms of money, you should be committing your budget towards the things that you and your partner decide are actually going to be adding real and lasting value to your wedding day.

This doesn't mean that you need to remortgage your house and jeopardise the future of any potential offspring in order to pay for every last thing that might carry any value to you on your wedding day. The disadvantages of debt, or of losing anything that is of value to you in your life beyond your wedding day, in fact changes the value of anything you want at your wedding. If you know that hiring an Austin Healey to transport you to your venue will make it difficult and stressful to afford food for the next year, then why not consider arriving in your clapped-out Ford Focus? Everyone who knows and loves you most, i.e. your wedding guests, will be more likely to beam fondly as you arrive, appreciating your frugal and courageous character, than to feel any criticism of your choice of transport.

In short: careful consideration of cost versus value, and tweaking your budget allocation, will help you to create the ideal day for you and one that your guests will remember for ever, for all the right reasons.

EXERCISE 6
FIVE-MINUTE WEDDING DECISIONS

Without wanting to state the obvious, planning a wedding isn't easy. There are so many ideas, things, people and other variables to consider that it can seem like a miracle when things finally fall into place.

This exercise is designed to help you and your partner decide – within only five minutes for each item you are considering – what is actually going to be valuable to you at your wedding. For anything you're considering for

CHAPTER 3 – WANTING AND NEEDING

your wedding day, you only need to answer five questions, write a short statement and give a score out of 10. Whenever you and your partner give different scores out of 10, simply add the two scores together and divide by two, giving your average score.

1. What is the value to you and your partner?
2. What is the value to your wedding guests?
3. What is the value to your wedding day?
4. What is the value in terms of memorability?
5. How important is it to use a professional?

To avoid any doubt about how this might work, I have created two examples, with my own corresponding judgments on value. Please don't allow my opinions to influence yours – values are highly subjective and there's nothing wrong if yours are very different from mine.

Example 1: Buying a wedding dress

1. What is the value to you and your partner?
   To the bride, this probably means looking your very best – whether like a princess, the picture of sophistication or a bohemian bride – depending on your own preferences. The value is you looking and feeling a million dollars. The dress is also always going to be one of the most talked-about things, not only on the day but afterwards.
   For your partner the value is in seeing you as you

want to be seen – beautiful, confident and radiant. I would therefore give this value a score of 10 out of 10.

2. What is the value to your guests?
   Similar to your partner in some respects, in that they will be enjoy seeing someone they love as the picture of confidence and perfection.
   Again, I think 10 is a safe bet for this value score.

3. What is the value to your wedding day?
   As mentioned above, the dress is one of the most talked-about things from a wedding day. While guests are waiting for the bride to arrive at the ceremony, a lot of the talk will be about the bride and what she'll be wearing. It is something that sets the tone of the day and will be seen in the majority of the photos.
   Value score – 10, surely.

4. What is the value in terms of memorability?
   Again, the dress will be one of the most memorable things, so its value is going to be pretty high. Without wanting to stereotype, I think it's safe to say that many of the women will probably remember the dress as by Stella York, with a sweetheart top and intricate flowery lace detail around the hem, while the blokes will remember it was white (if you're lucky). But as a couple, you will never forget how you looked, and you'll never forget how it felt

to be in that dress and how it felt to see your partner's reaction.

So it's going to be a score of 10.

5. How important is it to use a professional?
I'll cover other examples later about when and how you could save yourself a fortune by creating something yourself or going for a cheaper option. For your wedding dress, though, unless you are skilled enough to make your own, then using a professional is pretty important in order to ensure high quality, comfort and any necessary adjustments being made accurately and professionally.
This and a whole bunch of other things bring us to a firm score of 10.

We now add these scores – tough maths coming up . . .

10 + 10 +10 + 10 + 10 = 50

We now check this score against the following bandings:

0–15: Pointless

16–25: If budget allows, but consider the cheapest option

26–32: Worth considering

33–40: Make budget allow if possible

41–50: VITAL

As you see, any score of 41–50 is considered VITAL for your wedding.

A beautiful wedding dress, which the bride loves, provided by a professional: VITAL. Now, who would have thought that?

Example 2: Booking a wedding magician

I'm not going to give any apology for this potentially sounding like a sales pitch. The same arguments as I've given below would apply to any type of entertainer you are considering for your wedding, but I'm not familiar enough with the pros and cons of other entertainers to be able to give a full evaluation. You can therefore simply substitute any type of entertainer into this example as you read it through. I am, funnily enough, very familiar with the different aspects of value that I or my many magician friends bring to weddings, so here's my breakdown:

1. What is the value to you and your partner?
   First of all, the magician will perform tricks to you as a couple, so there's the enjoyment factor for you, but usually the biggest chunk of value will be in avoiding awkward lulls during the day. You can then, for example, go and have your photos taken after the ceremony without feeling you're abandoning your guests, allowing you to relax into the photos rather than feeling you have to rush back. You don't need to worry about guests being bored or making small talk during the wedding breakfast, because the magician spots that and gets everyone laughing out loud. A good magician won't only be

CHAPTER 3 – WANTING AND NEEDING

there to perform magic – he or she will break the ice, get everyone talking and offer you the option of acting as MC, getting everyone's attention whenever needed and announcing your arrival, to thunderous applause, at the wedding breakfast. That plus seeing some fun, out-of-this-world magic, and being left with impossible souvenirs and memories from the day.

Possibly biased, but going also on the reactions from the couples I've performed for, I have to give this 10/10.

2. What is the value to your guests?
    In this example, the value to the guests reflects the answers to the first question. Instead of being left to stand around chatting to people, most of whom you don't know, you've got an entertainer who is breaking the ice, stopping the uncomfortable silences and giving you talking points. Instead of two hours feeling neglected during the photos, you feel special because the couple has shown how much they value you by investing in entertainment. You're also experiencing some hilarious and impossible magic and mind reading.

    How much does that mean to you? It's just got to be a 10.

3. What is the value to your wedding day?
    Setting a fun, light-hearted tone, keeping the day flowing perfectly from one part to the next, ice

broken between people that don't know each other, lulls turned into talking points and everyone talking about the wedding for months after.
Has to be 10 out of 10, right?

4. What is the value in terms of memorability?
I know I've been half-joking with the 10s but this is one that is a definite 10 for me. When was the last time you left a wedding and were raving about the colour of the seat covers a month later? And how long after the wedding do you find yourself thinking about how good the chicken was at the wedding breakfast? When I perform, I create moments in time that people simply don't forget, when things happen that are both hilarious and inexplicable, which stick with them for years.
Up to you on this one, but I really would have to give this a 10.

5. How important is it to use a professional?
In magic there will always be someone who will perform for less, so what does paying for a true professional get you? First off, the practical side: a professional magician will have public liability insurance (for up to £10 million). It gets you the experience of someone who has performed at hundreds of events – I've dealt with every type of heckler and tricky situation you can possibly imagine, I know how to split my time to ensure I get around all the guests so that no one misses out, I know how to

CHAPTER 3 – WANTING AND NEEDING

adapt my act to suit any audience or guest, and I can get the attention of all the guests in the room whenever you need me to. If by any chance I'm ill or injured and can't perform, I can call on one of the many other professional magicians I know and trust, who will cover for me with no alterations or hassle for your day – the same definitely can't be said for an amateur. So, unless you're happy with a bloke-who-does-a-few-tricks-at-the-pub-type magician, then using a professional is vital. I'll leave you to give this a score.

I have gone into a lot of depth on both of these examples to explain my reasons for the answers and scores. When you go through the questions for anything you are considering, you'll only need to write a brief statement summing up your thoughts on the value/importance and giving you a total score out of 50. I'll repeat the score banding here for easy reference:

0–15: Pointless

16–25: If budget allows / consider the cheapest option

26–32: Worth considering

33–40: Make budget allow if possible

41–50: VITAL

If anything comes in at under 30, I'd urge you to ask yourself why you are considering putting money towards it. I have used only two important examples above, but I can bet you will be surprised if you complete this exercise for all optional extras such as wedding favours, personalised napkins or a highly trained owl sweeping down to deliver the rings to the altar. If you're still convinced that you have *got* to have something which has scored low in value, here are some possible arguments that might still make you realise your wedding day will survive without it:

Because it's tradition to have it? Nonsense – break the mould and be yourself.

Because other people would be upset if you didn't have it? Remember, you're not in control of other people's thoughts and feelings, and you can't please everyone. This is *your* day.

Because you think it'd be cool/cute? Cool and cute are good, but genuine value is better.

Because I want it, alright? Okay, but if it doesn't hold much value, you can't surely want it that much. You could instead focus on feeling grateful for all the other things.

Crunch time

We have already established pretty plainly that there are very few things that you actually *need* for your wedding and everything else is just a *want*. However, not many people will opt to get married with no friends or family present. Hey, how likely is it that anyone planning a

Gretna Green wedding will have bought this book, let alone read this far? So, you are of course going to have unnecessary extras at your wedding, and this chapter's primary goal was to teach you the difference between wanting and needing, promoting the importance of value, and helping you to let go of anything that doesn't provide true value.

Here's the crux: the more value something has to you, the closer it is going to be to an actual need.

I hope that the last exercise will have helped you to determine how much value different things have to your day.

This next exercise is very simple. You will need two pieces of paper and a pen.

EXERCISE 7
WANTING AND NEEDING

At the top of one piece of paper write "WANT" and at the top of the other write "NEED". Think about all of the different products/services/suppliers you are considering for your big day and write them down on the appropriate sheets of paper.

Once this is complete, hide the "WANT" page away somewhere and don't look at it again until you have sorted out everything you need for your "NEED" list, which gives you your main priorities in terms of money, importance and urgency.

Once you have all your needs sorted out, you will be in a much stronger position to re-evaluate your wants. Not only will you know clearly how much budget you have left, but your clever brain will have been doing all sorts of work in the background, determining the importance and value of each of the items on your "WANT" list.

Conclusion on wanting and needing

> "Curb your desire – don't set your heart on so many things and you will get what you need."
>
> Epictetus

Wanting and needing are two entirely different things, and truly understanding the difference is a wonderful skill to have, especially when it comes to wedding planning. The higher the value you place on something, the closer it becomes to being a need. If something has little or no value to your wedding day, that defines it as a want.

Being a Stoic Bride will empower you to:

- Fully comprehend the differences between wanting and needing

- Understand and prioritise what you truly *need* at your wedding

- Accept how value is different from cost
- Focus your attention on the things that will add true value to your wedding, while cutting out some of the things that hold little value

CHAPTER 4
Giving permission

Eleanor Roosevelt, First Lady of the United States of America from 1933 to 1945, was a remarkable woman, who was not afraid to go against the grain and stand up for what she believed in, even when her beliefs were controversial. She's famous for a number of things, and one of her best-known quotes is something you've probably heard before. I love this quote so much, and I don't think there could be a better one for this section of the book.

> "No one can make you feel inferior without your consent"
>
> Eleanor Roosevelt

There have been several misquotations, or perhaps derivations, such as "No one can insult you without your consent" and "No one can make you feel bad without your permission". They all carry the same connotations, though.

Relating this back to Stoicism: anyone who says anything to you needs to be treated as an external influence, meaning you have absolutely no control over anything they say. The same applies if the situation is reversed – other people have no control over what you say.

What you do have control over is how you respond to this external influence. I'm in a perhaps enviable position, where practising this has made me incredibly good at it; I find that the only time an insult or hurtful remark actually makes me feel inferior, bad or upset is when I know there's an element (or a lot of) truth to it. In those cases, I see the comment only as a helpful reminder of something I need to work on improving. And, on the occasions when I have really mucked up, there has been no one more insulting or judging of my actions than me.

Let's think first about those instances when there isn't even an element of truth to an insult directed at you, or something that's been said at your expense.

Opinions and entitlement, enabling, validation, projection and permission

Well, first of all, people are entitled to their opinion, so you can just accept it and leave it at that (remembering what you can control). You didn't ask for their opinion but you've been given it, and it is worth exactly the same amount of money that you paid for it. Nothing.

It might be slightly harder not to become upset when you have actually asked for someone's opinion and their answer has not been what you wanted to hear.

Opinions and entitlement

Let us assume you're asking a friend about something you've got your heart set on for your wedding. Your friend is either going to agree with you, which gets you nowhere, or they're going to disagree with you, in which case you're running the risk of being upset by their response. And your friend is entitled to their opinion – you can't control that.

So, best-case scenario, you end up where you were before you started, with just one extra opinion backing up a decision you'd already made. Then, if your friend disagrees with you, you might end up in a pointless disagreement over something you're not going to shift from, but you're nevertheless left feeling slightly less positive about your decision.

This begs the question: why bother asking for someone's opinion if you've already decided what you want them to say? You have no control over their answer and there's only one answer that's going to be acceptable to you; what you're really looking for here is validation from an external source that your opinion is correct. Seeing as you have no control over their response and you've got your heart set on something, you're essentially setting yourself up for a fall.

You've got your heart set on the idea, so just do it.

A different situation might be where you're unsure about something for your wedding and are genuinely asking for an opinion from someone else. You then need to be willing to accept or at least consider the other person's opinion if you have asked for it. Even if you don't get the answer you were 100% hoping for, it's definitely still worth considering the other person's opinion.

Whether you are asking for a genuine opinion or validation of something you already have your heart set on, it's also important to remember that anyone you ask has two options when you ask them – being honest or dishonest. Honesty is of course the best policy, especially amongst friends. However, how many people will actually have the balls to be honest with a bride and tell her that her idea stinks? The answer to that question gives a clear indication of the likelihood of a truly valued response from someone else.

Enabling

Being dishonest when someone asks for your opinion makes you an "enabler". By not being 100% straight with someone about your thoughts, you are essentially

CHAPTER 4 – GIVING PERMISSION

giving the other person your "permission" to do something other than what you consider to be the best course of action.

You are trying to protect the other person from hurt in the short term, not to mention avoiding potential conflict with that person. Instead of "ripping off the plaster", i.e. being brutally honest but saving them from hurt further down the line, you'll be providing short-term gain for long-term pain. Remember, everyone is entitled to their opinions. You can of course be as tactful and sensitive as possible in delivering your opinion, but if someone has asked for your opinion, they have to be prepared to accept the answer they don't ideally want to hear.

In the long term, the effects of enabling someone can be anything from slightly adverse to very detrimental, especially when it comes to behaviour.

Imagine the following example: a close friend of yours, Mariana, has had a few dates with a guy. Things seemed to be going well and Mariana has been happier than you've seen her in a while, but now he has suddenly gone quiet. He hasn't explicitly called things off, but it's clear to you – especially after hearing a rumour or two from other friends – that the relationship has run its course. Mariana is starting to feel heartbroken at the prospect and she asks for your help: "I've sent Rafael a message every day for the last week and he hasn't responded to any of them. I can see that he read the first four but he hasn't even opened the next three. Do you think something's happened to him? Would I look crazy and needy if I messaged him again?"

You're torn. It seems very clear to you that, for whatever reason, former smooth operator Rafael is now being a douchebag by not being straight with Mariana. You also recognise that this is something neither you nor Mariana can control. Mariana probably does already appear needy and/or crazy to Rafael after continuing to message him every day – you have little doubt that she should give up and start to get over her sadly short-lived infatuation.

Let's look at two possible scenarios here.

Scenario 1

You can't bear to be the one to break Mariana's heart. You even justify this to yourself, "Who knows – they're probably only malicious rumours – maybe he's been struck down with a mystery illness". So, you reassure her that messaging him for only a week can't be seen as crazy or needy, and that she should trust her own instinct and keep trying until he tells her it's over.

Mariana's relief is almost tangible. She hugs you and thanks you for being such a good friend, and you're relieved to see her feeling so much happier again. Deep down, though, you know that this will only end in tears. You've just told Mariana that it's okay to keep sending messages to someone who's clearly uninterested, thereby enabling her to continue her needy/crazy behaviour. You've given her the green light to carry on.

You also know that you won't be surprised if two weeks later Mariana is asking, "Is it weird if I wait outside his house until he comes home and ask him why he hasn't responded to my messages?" You've set the trend by saying it's not weird and, before you know it, Rafael has put a restraining order on your friend, at which point Mariana finally comes to her senses . . . and gets angry at you for not telling her how weirdly she was acting.

Scenario 2

You've known Mariana for over ten years and really value her friendship, but you know she's not likely to take kindly to hearing the truth. Still, you can't bring yourself to let her potentially make a fool of herself with this Romeo Rafael. You take a deep breath, look her straight in the eye . . . and tell her she's acting like a needy/crazy person, and she needs to move on.

Mariana is mortified. This is definitely not what she was wanting to hear from you. "How could you say that? You're meant to be my friend!" After five minutes of arguing with you about why she's not crazy, then flouncing out and spending two days sulking at home, Mariana finally sees sense. She's cried out all her hurt, recognises Rafael as the ratbag he really is, and apologises for losing her rag with you. You and Mariana drink some gin and have a great night together, laughing your heads off about Rafael's terrible taste in clothes. After two days of worrying about falling out with your friend, you're pleasantly surprised to find that your relationship feels closer than ever.

There's actually a third scenario, which is the reason for this analogy . . .

As I mentioned at the start of this chapter, it's pointless to ask someone for their opinion if your mind is already made up. Whenever you ask for an opinion, you should be in a place where you're ready and willing to fully accept the response, rather than only seeking endorsement of your own decision.

If you are put in a position where you know, deep down, that the other person only really wants reassurance that they are right, as in the case of poor Mariana, your most powerful response might be to ask, "Have you already made up your mind on this?"

Now, it is still fairly likely that the other person won't already have accepted that to be the case. If they deny expecting a certain response, claiming that they honestly value your opinion, you could press further, for example, "How would you feel if I did say you should stop messaging Rafael?" That in itself should be enough to make Mariana realise she's not really giving you the option to tell her she is acting crazily. If she still insists that she needs to hear from you what she should do, it's probably time for you to resort to the brutally honest approach from Scenario 2, above.

CHAPTER 4 – GIVING PERMISSION

Whenever you are in the position of wanting to make powerful decisions for yourself, the next exercise will help you to do exactly that.

Returning to our earlier example, Mariana would actually have benefited from taking some time to ask herself for her own genuine and objective opinion. Her indecisiveness most likely stemmed from a lack of confidence. Her unwillingness to accept the truth of the situation was fuelled by her emotional needs, i.e. her desire for the relationship with Rafael to continue. Hey, if she'd been faced with a friend in the same situation, there's little doubt that Mariana would have recognised that the relationship was a lost cause.

Mariana could have saved herself further heartache and potential humiliation by looking for the answer in herself. After all, who could be more qualified to give the right answer, without any tactful cushioning? It was clear in this situation that she already subconsciously recognised the truth – why else would she have been asking you if she seemed needy or crazy?

True, Mariana found herself in a state of conflict. On one hand, there was a guy she really liked and wanted to have in her life, but there was also a part of her that knew full well that the relationship wasn't going anywhere and she was acting like a big pot of crazy. If she had genuinely sat down and allowed an honest and open inner dialogue, there is little doubt that Mariana could have stepped confidently away from the situation. Sure, she would have felt emotionally bruised, but she'd have had her head up high as she headed out for the next girls' night out, looking for someone altogether more worthwhile than old Rafael.

I firmly believe that everyone would benefit from talking to themselves more, both internally and out loud as well (but probably in the comfort of your own home rather than having a two-way argument with yourself on the Tube). This might sound like a weird thing to do, but I'm sure you're already seeing the potential benefits; it will only be a matter of time before it feels completely normal to you, and you can enjoy your new bolder, cleverer you.

The following is a great exercise, which can be used for any decision making that you have in your life. It's something Mariana would definitely have benefited from, but (sorry, Mariana) we're going to ditch her and go through this example as if it were a wedding decision you're trying to make. In short, it's a visualisation exercise, whereby you'll be imagining a situation and then removing yourself from it in order to gain a better perspective.

EXERCISE 8
DECISIONS BY DISSOCIATION

Let's say you're considering booking a popcorn stand for your wedding. It seems expensive for what it is, but you're also thinking that it would be a fun extra to your day. You've found one that virtually runs itself and even produces sweet and salty options. Something for everyone, right? You can see all the potential pros, but you're still not 100% sure whether the popcorn stand is worth the money.

You might be happy to keep your eyes closed, as suggested below, for this exercise. However, please don't feel you have to if that is difficult or uncomfortable in any way – you will still gain from the exercise if you follow it with your eyes open.

If you are happy to shut your eyes, you can simply read through the whole exercise a couple of times before starting, to memorise the steps (don't worry – the steps are logical and easy to remember). Or, if or when you are somewhere you can listen in peace to an audio recording, go to www.chrispiercymagic.co.uk/bwp-exercises to hear my extended explanation and recording of this exercise, which will be even easier to follow and more effective.

1. Find somewhere quiet and comfortable where you can sit without being disturbed

2. Close your eyes and begin by focusing on your breathing. Don't try to alter your breathing at all, just focus on it as you inhale and exhale

3. Start to notice the changes that your breathing causes, for example the rising and falling of your

chest, and the different sensations as your lungs fill with air and then empty again

4. Begin to become aware of your thoughts. As soon as you notice a new thought, don't make any judgments on it at all – just accept what you are thinking and let the thought pass. You can start to recognise your passing thoughts for exactly what they are – thoughts that are temporarily in your mind, which you simply don't need to do anything about at this moment

5. Continue this awareness until your mind feels clear. Still, for the rest of this exercise, don't feel bad if another thought enters your mind – simply recognise it as a thought and let it go again, allowing yourself to come back to the exercise

6. Now imagine that you're not sitting where you are right now, but in your own private cinema. Take a little time to imagine the details of your new environment – the comforting atmosphere; the colours, fabrics and darkness of the cinema; the feeling of the seat beneath you; the empty seats around you. Then look ahead, where you see a large cinema screen directly in front of you

7. Begin to imagine that the film you're about to watch is actually your wedding day, however you're not seeing the day through your own eyes. You're seeing this in full 4D, as if you were a fly on a wall,

able to go anywhere and see anything without being noticed

8. Bring your wedding to life in all its glory but without the popcorn stand in place. Imagine everything you have planned for your wedding day – the colours, the sights, the sounds, the people, the smells, the tastes of the food - everything. Really engage with your imagination, allowing it to run wild so that you can enjoy the feeling of your beautiful wedding day, with everything running smoothly

9. Now imagine your big day as a short film clip, which has been carefully edited to only about one minute long. You'll be able to run that clip through in your mind, while still experiencing all the other senses of your wedding. Imagine that film clip up on the screen right in front of you now – it hasn't started playing yet – it will begin whenever you are ready to see it. Mentally make any final adjustments to the film in terms of brightness, colours, feelings, tastes, etc, until it feels just right

10. Now start to imagine you're watching this clip play out. You can see, feel, taste, smell and touch every last detail of your wedding, all concentrated into just one minute. Notice how this makes you feel; notice the impact that it has on all of your senses

11. Once the clip has been played through, imagine you can instantly rewind it and start it again. Play

the clip through at least twice more – it is important to get a real feel of exactly what your day will be like

12. With your wedding day clearly in your mind, now play through the clip again, but with one difference: now there is also the popcorn stand, exactly where you imagined it being placed
    - How does your wedding look different?
    - How does it feel different?
    - How much impact does the popcorn stand have?
    - What does it change?
    - How different is everything at the wedding now that the popcorn stand is there?

13. With this slightly tweaked film clip available to watch, play it through fully two or three times in your mind, exactly as you did before, to really lock the idea of it into your head

14. With the two clips now firmly in your mind, you have clearly imagined the two distinct scenarios
    Was your wedding better with the popcorn stand? If yes, how much better?
    Did the popcorn stand add value to you, your guests and your wedding? If yes, how much value? Does the value of the popcorn stand outweigh the costs?

15. Make your decision. You now know all you need to know, so just make the decision, stick to it and

feel happy with your decision. Take all the time you need to make this decision and then begin to reacquaint yourself with your real-life surroundings. When you are ready, open your eyes

Give yourself permission to trust your own decisions – this is an incredibly powerful and self-esteem-boosting skill. Once you've learnt the skill, I really hope that you'll no longer feel the need to seek validation from external sources, and that you'll be able to make good, strong, informed and *independent* decisions for your wedding and for your life.

This doesn't mean that you're never permitted to ask for other people's opinions, but that you don't need to every single time, least of all when you want to feel in control of any situation and any decision.

Projection

We started this chapter with the quote from Eleanor Roosevelt, "No one can make you feel inferior without your consent".

One of the times we are most likely to allow people to make us feel inferior is when we don't fully understand the reasons for their words or actions. This is something we have doubtless all experienced, when someone makes us feel unrealistically negative about ourselves, or about someone or something else, due to negative circumstances or conditions in their own life.

In psychology, this is known as "projection". Psychological projection is, at its core, a defence mechanism, which usually works on a subconscious level. It is used by people who feel unable to cope with negative feelings or emotions, which they themselves are experiencing. Rather than admitting those negative feelings to themselves, they "project" them onto other people, thereby reducing the fallout of the negative feelings on themselves.

Some examples of projection

- A cheating husband who, due to his own infidelity, develops groundless distrust of his wife. He starts to monitor her behaviour, constantly looking for signs of betrayal and accusing her of cheating, all because he's unable to face up to what he has done. At the start, the wife might even feel flattered by his protective jealousy, thereby unconsciously giving him consent to judge and criticise her. It is often only once the relationship is beyond repair that she recognises the dangers of the initial signals of distrust.

- Very similar circumstances can develop when the husband has been the victim of cheating in a previous relationship. Either of these first two examples is of course just as likely to happen to either person, regardless of gender or sexuality. They're just examples.

- The woman who is so insecure about how she looks that she insults other people's looks, whether to their face or behind their back, to make herself feel better about her own appearance.

I'm sure you're getting the idea of this now. There's also positive projection, which is of course a whole lot friendlier, but that is not relevant to this chapter. We're talking here about how you can protect yourself from negative projection from others.

Ask yourself where's it's coming from

The next time someone says something unpleasant to you or does something unkind, give yourself a moment to think about what's been said or done, and why that person might have acted in that way. First of all, you can of course remind yourself that this is outside your sphere of influence and that they're entitled to their opinions. But, especially if the other person is being hurtful towards you, it is also helpful to delve deeper. Ask yourself, "Why are they saying that about me? Where has it come from? Is this actually only about how they feel about themselves?"

Admittedly, in the words of Batman's butler in *The Dark Knight*, "Some people just want to watch the world burn" – there are people out there who just enjoy being unkind or destructive. But I think you would be surprised by how many more people are hurting inside and don't know how to deal with the hurt, and their rude comments and actions are simply by-products of their pain and feelings of inadequacy.

You must have at least one friend, who you know has at least one hang-up, which makes them take things the wrong way and/or say hurtful things. If, for example, your friend's mother used to become physically aggressive when she (regularly) drank alcohol, you would forgive your friend for a snide remark as you headed up to the bar to order your third drink.

What I'm asking you to do, which might not immediately come easily, is to show exactly the same empathy towards *anyone* else who says something critical or hurtful. There simply must be a reason for them feeling and acting that way. You know their remarks are unfounded, so you can only feel empathy for them due to whatever they have experienced. If their remark was particularly hurtful or inappropriate, you might simply try to take what they've said and think to yourself, "I'm sorry that you feel that way about yourself".

As soon as you have become used to feeling this way about hurtful comments, you will start to feel a lot stronger

CHAPTER 4 – GIVING PERMISSION

and more positive in yourself. You are no longer giving people consent to make you feel inferior. Eleanor Roosevelt would be proud of you.

Here's the particular power of this skill in relation to your wedding. You are very likely going to be coming together with a lot of people you don't see on a daily basis, and a lot of those people will be coming from a place of insecurity, especially at a happy and beautiful wedding. This might be due to their own failed marriages, their financial insecurity, or the fact that your wedding is more enjoyable than they think theirs was.

The list is endless – weddings evoke an endless outpouring of love and positivity, but they can also trigger some negative emotions from just a few people. Without preparing yourself with this chapter, it's likely you'll feel so hurt by one or two negative comments, you'll find yourself thinking more about those than the heaps of positive feedback from others.

If someone says something at your wedding is rubbish, pointless or a waste of money, it could be coming from anywhere at all. If you simply accept before your wedding day (why not now?) that there will of course be some negative comments, but that they will be only a reflection of the people making them, you will be able to smile sympathetically and enjoy your wedding just as much as if those comments had never been made.

To reiterate, in order to deal with any negative comments, remember the following things:

- Someone's actions and comments are not within your sphere of influence

- Someone's actions and comments are often a reflection of how they feel about themselves

- Some people – luckily very few – are just unkind

Give yourself permission to understand where other people's thoughts and actions might be coming from, and you will protect yourself from unnecessary anguish.

Ronan was wrong

Ronan Keating famously sang "Life is a Rollercoaster". I have to tell you that he is completely wrong. I apologise in advance to any of his lifelong fans – this isn't personal.

The song itself expands on its title: "Life is a rollercoaster, just gotta ride it". Don't worry – I get the metaphor – life has its ups and downs and you've got to stick with it, knowing that some parts of life are good and some are bad.

For a start, the metaphor is flawed because the downs on a rollercoaster are typically the most exciting parts, whereas the ups are the parts where tension, anticipation and anxiety are built up. The opposite of life's ups and downs. Either way, Ronan was wrong – life is not a rollercoaster.

> SIDE NOTE: Whilst we're dispelling metaphors for life, I need to point out that life is not like a box of chocolates, either. Every box of chocolates has an index card to allow you to choose the chocolate that you like. What sort of monster goes with pot luck in a box of Quality Street?

Why life isn't a rollercoaster

I'm clear about life having its ups and downs, of which everyone has their share. But insisting that it's a rollercoaster, which you've just got to ride, implies that you have no control over the ups and downs or how they affect you, because you are rigidly fixed in your seat, inside a car on a track, over which you have no control. It gives the impression that you are somehow locked into the events that are happening around you, with no power over their consequences.

Life could be described as a rollercoaster if – and only if – we let everything in life happen to us, while allowing everything in and around our lives to affect us as much as those events possibly could. But what about control? What about our sphere of influence? What about us choosing to work towards tranquillity?

There will admittedly be a few events within our lifetime that are going to take us for a ride on this so-called rollercoaster, when we'll find it difficult or problematic to get off the ride. For example, losing a loved one or friend will always affect you, unless you take your Stoicism to such an extreme that you're living by the other definition of stoicism, i.e. being emotionless and utterly resilient.

Upon hearing of the death of his son in battle, one Roman commander from the school of Stoicism told the messenger, "I did not think I begat an immortal", i.e. "He was only human – he had to die at some point". Some people might view that as impressive emotional restraint, but for me that is just too cold. I firmly believe we need to accept and live by our human emotions in order to fully enjoy life; I'll get back to that point in the final three chapters.

For me, grief will always ensure that we remain emotionally attached to the event. Such strong emotions attach themselves to other significant events – both happy and sad – such as becoming a parent, gaining a degree, being involved in a car accident or being fired from work. However, beyond such life-altering events, which force us at least initially into an emotional response, we do actually have choice. We find ourselves in positions where WE decide how much we are going to allow external events to affect us. We decide how much *permission* we give to those events.

A better, and more Stoical, metaphor for life

I feel it would be pretty naughty of me to debunk one metaphor (actually, two so far) without putting one forward myself, so here's mine: Life is like flying a big kite in random weather conditions.

I'll admit that it's not as catchy as Ronan's and I'd be impressed if someone could make a hit record from it, but the metaphor is solid.

Why life is like flying a big kite in random weather conditions

Being on a rollercoaster means you have no control at all over what you're doing or how you're feeling – you are quite literally strapped in and along for the ride. Flying a kite is completely different. While you can't control the weather itself, you CAN control your own actions.

If the air is too still to shift even the smallest feather, you can always opt to drive somewhere more gusty, climb a hill until you find a breeze, or enlist a friend to hold the kite up while you run fast enough to get the kite in the air.

If there's a good wind but it keeps changing, you also retain the choice over how much you allow the weather conditions to affect the kite and your enjoyment. Although you have an attachment to the kite itself as it blusters around in the breeze, you can let the line out or draw it in, thereby controlling how the kite reacts.

Then, imagine one day you are out having the best kite-flying session ever with a bunch of good friends, when a massive, unexpected storm kicks in. You suddenly find yourself desperately hanging onto the kite spool, you somehow can't control the length of your line, and worse still, you look round to find that all your friends have run for cover. This is the closest the kite gets to the roller-coaster metaphor.

There are, sadly, some times in life where you suddenly feel isolated from others and lacking in control – those times when a really negative event forces itself on you – and where you need to hang on for dear life and wait for the storm to pass.

At any other time while flying a kite, though, you will always have some control. You'll have some beautifully sunny days, with just enough breeze to keep the kite happily floating above you. There will be those days when the wind is so strong, you have to use all your skill to keep the line the right length and your kite from getting tangled, but you enjoy the adrenaline of the challenge. I like the idea of there being no breeze at all, where you are forced to run as fast as you can, until you are exhausted but exhilarated to see the kite flying high. I am sure you can tell which stages and states of life I'm referring to with these metaphors within the metaphor, and I'm sure you can think of some other kite-flying states that relate to other events and emotions.

I hope you can see that this is an altogether sounder and healthier metaphor for life and that Ronan was definitely wrong.

Conclusion on giving permission

Permission applies to a whole range of different aspects of our life. In this context, we are talking about allowing ourselves to trust in our decisions and believe in our choices and, more importantly, to have enough about ourselves to decide what we are and are not going to allow to affect us.

We have looked at how everyone is entitled to their own opinions; we can't control those opinions, but we can control their potential effects on us. We've talked about why we don't always need to seek others' advice, and how we can give other people permission to take certain actions, enabling them to do something, which so often isn't the best course of action. I've touched on how others might attempt to project negative emotions onto you, and how you can withstand those emotions by empathising with the other person's situation. And I hope that I have illustrated clearly why you don't need to see your life as a scary rollercoaster over which you have no control. If yes, you are one big step nearer to your tranquil state of mind.

Being a Stoic Bride will empower you to:

- Accept that others are entitled to their opinions, but that they don't need to affect you

- Not feel obliged to enable other people

- Permit yourself to trust your decisions, without needing to ask for others' opinions

- Understand that you can give permission for external events to affect you or not

- Accept that some of the events in your life will be so life-changing that your tranquillity will, temporarily, be altered

- Appreciate that you have control over how everything else affects you

CHAPTER 5
Amor fati

> "Some of the best things that have ever happened to us wouldn't have happened to us, if it weren't for some of the worst things that have ever happened to us."
>
> Mokokoma Mokhonoana

For those of us not schooled in Latin (which includes me), "amor fati" can be translated as "love of fate", or perhaps "accept and loving everything that happens".

In essence, amor fati is an attitude in which someone is completely accepting of everything that happens in life, accepting that everything that happens is good, or at worst necessary.

And yes, before you ask, this encompasses everything, including suffering and loss. So, whilst no one is ever going to ask you to "love" the fact that your wedding dress caught fire or someone broke their leg on the dancefloor at your wedding, the concept of amor fati asks you to accept that it has happened and to let it affect your tranquillity as little as possible.

I will again point out that we will be going into further detail about emotions and feelings with regards to Stoicism in the final three chapters.

Does bad mean bad?

I'm really not a big fan of the expression "everything happens for a reason". I do appreciate its meaning and positive aspirations, but it is all too often used as a throwaway comment, which people use when something rubbish has happened for which they have no real understanding or perspective.

Worse still is "It's all part of God's plan", which similarly removes any onus on anyone to do anything – there's apparently some plan you're unaware of, which removes any ability to change the situation. I hate the lack of pragmatism here, and despise the thought that we're supposed just to sit and wait for the good to work its way out of any bad situation.

> SIDE NOTE: This is not a slight on religion at all.

Whoever you are, wherever you've been, whatever you've done, whomever you know, the fact is that lousy situations are going to present themselves in your life. Some will be mindblowing, out-of-the-blue and catastrophic events, which you simply have no hope of understanding. Some will be mild inconveniences, of which some people will experience a lot, while other people will experience fewer. However, I don't think anyone is immune from "fate" (for want of a better word).

Loved ones will pass, accidents will happen. The kindest, most honest people will contract awful illnesses. Whether you want to call this "bad luck" or "just what happens in life" is pretty irrelevant – either way, bad things will to happen to all of us at some points in life.

> ANOTHER SIDE NOTE: I really hate how depressing this sounds but it is a necessary evil that needs to be discussed.

So, what then – just sit around miserably, knowing that awful things are going to happen? Absolutely not.

Having read this far in the book, you'll hopefully have a good idea about what is coming next. Remember, it isn't what happens around us that should affect how we feel, but how we respond to those happenings.

Imagine your house burns down. Afterwards, do you mourn the loss of your home and belongings, or do you celebrate that fact you got out alive, with a new-found love of every new day? Do you recognise the opportunity to potentially improve your living situation? What will be the most important things in your life after it happens? (Remember the survivors of Hurricane Katrina.)

The rings get lost on your wedding day, delaying the ceremony by an hour. Do you chastise the incompetent ring-bearer for being so stupid and inconsiderate? Or do you laugh it off, enjoy your day and just feel content that your happily-ever-after was delayed by only one hour?

As I learn more and grow older (and perhaps wiser), I'm really doing my best to try not to categorise things as "good" or "bad", or as "right" or "wrong". Right and wrong are much better replaced with "helpful to the situation" and "unhelpful to the situation". Right and wrong are not only subjective – they are also automatically linked to some form of judgment, blaming and, as a result, guilt.

Good and bad are similarly unhelpful terms. If something is good, we have to be happy about it, right? And by contrast we must be sad when bad things happen, correct? What if you could look at a situation and, rather than thinking it is good or bad, you simply accepted that it just IS – "it is what it is". This doesn't mean that nothing can be done about it, though.

> SIDE NOTE: This isn't banning the words good, bad, right and wrong, or trying to redefine their meanings. You'll be able to find plenty of times I've used those words throughout this book. I'm

> talking here only of when it can be unhelpful to resolutely categorise things that happen to us as purely positive or negative.

Falling into the habit of categorising something as a good thing or a bad thing doesn't change what the thing is. Instead, it takes whatever it is and almost forces a particular response to it, based on the category into which it has been placed.

Bad is only bad if you decide that it is bad.

> "Seek not for events to happen as you wish but rather wish for events to happen as they do, and your life will go smoothly."
>
> Epictetus

The ONLY game

Some people like to ponder on the possibility of there being parallel universes.

Have you ever made an important decision and wondered how your life would have been if you'd decided differently? You may even have considered a parallel life, in which everything is affected, depending on any number of decisions you have made.

You might have seen the film *Sliding Doors*, in which we see the life of the main character running in two very different directions. Helen, played by Gwyneth Paltrow, gets fired from work and catches a train home, only to find her boyfriend in bed with another woman. Then we see a parallel scenario, where Helen misses that train and arrives home after the other woman has left. Helen's life is then played out in both directions, leading to very different circumstances and outcomes.

This film illustrates how one tiny delay can lead to a very different version of your life. And it can be argued that even smaller events could have similar outcomes. You might, say, be currently living in Universe A because you chose chocolate sprinkles on your mocha back in 2015, while there's another version of you in Universe B who decided against them.

Now, while it can be interesting to consider a million "what ifs" and their potential impacts, it's crazy to expend any serious levels of thought and energy on this. While it might be fun to think, "I wonder where I'd be if I hadn't met my partner" and there's a certain romance to it, it's more pertinent to think here about those people (and maybe you're one of them) who lose sleep over the decisions they've made or the situations they now find themselves in.

Let's assume there is a parallel universe somewhere out there with another version of you. Is their situation any different or did things work out the same? Has a significant event changed them as a person at all? Is the person you are now even able to become this other version of you, knowing what has happened in Universe A? Do you have any idea if they're in any better situation at all? I'm talking evidence, not guesswork. And the answer, quite simply, is that you don't know.

Finally, and most importantly . . .

Would you ever be able to swap places with the other you, living in that other universe? Answer: NO.

Stoics are famously fatalistic, by which I mean that they accept what has occurred, focusing only on the present and what is in their control.

The past is not in our control – what has happened has happened.

The ONLY game you have to play is the one you are playing right here, right now: your life, your circumstances, your decisions; your feelings, thoughts and actions.

So, even if there is a second Janet (or whatever your name is), with a better life, more money and a happier relationship in a different universe – who cares? You are your own Janet – comparing yourself with anyone, let alone an imaginary version of yourself, is pointless, unhelpful and is ONLY ever going to bring frustration and hurt.

Love your fate. Make a decision right now to love – yes, LOVE – everything that happens to you. All of the perceived good, all of the perceived bad and everything in between. Because all of this "stuff" is going to happen, so you might as well greet it all in the best way you possibly can, which is with acceptance.

By choosing acceptance and love of your situation, you position yourself in the absolute best place to make a decision about how you are going to react to your circumstances. This is clearly a particularly powerful place to be when you are deciding how to react to very testing and difficult situations – the more upsetting the situation, the more important it is to be accepting of it. Even though you will be looking for ways to move on from a negative situation, you can simply accept it until then, rather than collapsing under the strain. And instead of flat-out denying what is happening to you, accepting it will strengthen your position in finding a way out.

This doesn't mean you are never allowed to get emotional, be upset, cry, scream, fight or feel rage – you are human, after all. But your reaction from the point when the emotion has cleared (or at least subsided somewhat) is much easier to make from this place of acceptance.

The long game

No one likes stubbing their toe. It's one of the most infuriating things conceivable – right up there with accidentally biting the inside of your cheek. All you can do is curse the heavens, use any combination of expletives that seems fitting, and swear (in vain) that you'll never do it again. This is very much a short-term suffering, in which there's little chance of these heartfelt intentions having any protracted projection on our futures.

What about missing a flight? Losing a job? Having a wedding supplier go out of business? How did you meet your partner? How did you meet your best friend? What sparked your interest in the things you are now most passionate about in life? Why is your favourite flower the one that it is?

Who we are; what we have done; what we like, hate and find funny – all those things have been shaped by the situations, good and bad, which have unfolded around us. Missing a flight might have felt infuriating at the time, but it may also have altered your life to the point where the ensuing course of events led you to meeting your partner. Losing your job might have caused you to reach out to old friends and reconnect, causing a rediscovered passion for cross-stitch, which is now the basis of your thriving new business.

I don't believe there are lines directly between events, nor do I think that anyone or anything has a plan or route set out for our lives; as humans, we and our lives are much too complicated for this to be true. I do firmly believe, however, that any situation or decision, however large or small, has the potential of leading to a significant change within our lives. It's entirely possible that what you consider the worst thing that's ever happened to you actually directly led to what you consider the best thing, or even vice versa. But there's little or no chance of ever being able to be 100% certain that A caused B, or D caused E, or whatever caused whatever else.

As humans, we tend to like patterns, and we mentally draw lines between situations. However, these lines are rarely drawn based on any cast-iron evidence or proof; they are drawn because they fit in with the stories that we tell ourselves. Those stories rarely contain all the facts, almost always have the corners shaved off to make them sound more interesting or more fitting, and almost always put us in the most or the least favourable light, depending on our personal dispositions. (More on the stories we tell ourselves in Chapter 8.)

This again leads me back to acceptance and amor fati. One lousy incident is never an excuse for a bad life – you always have choices and you can decide how you respond to things. A difficult situation might become the best thing ever because of the strength, courage or goodwill that it brings about. For example, the trauma of desperately trying to save someone's life often inspires a person to become a medical professional.

Being in a serious accident can be the catalyst for becoming an organ donor. Losing a best friend to suicide almost always causes the bonds between those that loved that person to strengthen (and I'm wiping a genuine tear from my eye while typing this – RIP, Tom).

You are playing the ONLY game there is to play and the game is a long one. Accept all the situations and events that crop up, and resolve to use them to your advantage.

Obstacles are opportunities

I could write a whole book on this subject. I won't, however, as that has already been done and much better than I could ever write it (read *The Obstacle is the Way* by Ryan Holiday).

Some of the greatest people in history have been borne out of adversity, some of the greatest products were created entirely by accident, and many of the strongest relationships are forged in the fire of the most painful losses.

Prison is a great example of what can be achieved, depending on the mindset adopted. Let's imagine that you suddenly find yourself in jail. It's slowly dawning on you that a) you shouldn't have thrown that stapler at Barbara in Accounts Receivable, and b) it might have been wise to invest in a stronger lawyer. You've been convicted of GBH with intent and are facing a 10-year jail sentence with no chance of parole . . . your next 10 years are definitely going to be spent in a jail cell.

What next?

Well, you could, if you like, spend 10 years plotting your next big diamond heist with your new-found connections in prison.

OR

You could spend each minute of every day of your jail sentence planning your revenge on those who wronged you and put you behind bars.

OR

Amor fati – you could decide to fall in love with what fate has brought you. Fate has delivered you an opportunity. You have 10 years, a lot of which you will spend alone – what are you going to do with all this time you've been gifted? Want that absolutely ripped physique? You've got several hours every day to smash out cardio and bodyweight exercises. Want to learn everything there is to know about quantum mechanics? The prison's library can get you any book. Want to do a degree so you have improved career prospects when you are released? You've certainly got the time for that now.

Stormy weather

Your wedding day is, potentially, the happiest day of your life. You've arranged for it to take place on a Saturday in July, when the weather is nearly always tremendous. This gives you the confidence that you will have glorious sunshine and perfect light all day, especially for the all-important photos around the grounds of your luxury wedding venue. On Friday night, the forecast for the following day is perfect and, glancing out of the window just before you go to sleep, you can see there isn't a cloud in the sky. Then the next morning you awake to a thunderstorm and the weather forecast saying there is a 100% chance of rain all day.

This isn't bad – this is *dreadful*, right?

Wrong.

Remember that it is so much more beneficial for us to think of things in terms of things being helpful or unhelpful, as opposed to right or wrong.

Is it helpful for it to be hammering it down on your wedding day?

No.

Is it terminal for your wedding day?

Only if it is so bad that the wedding is cancelled by the venue; otherwise no, unless you decide to make it terminal.

Here's where your preparation comes into play. Did you blindly go into your summer wedding day, naively thinking that the weather was definitely going to be fine? Or did you consider what would happen if there was light drizzle, a heavy downpour or an all-day thunderstorm? If you have completed the preparation work described in Chapter

2 on control, you will be in the best possible situation to deal with any circumstance that arises. However, you still have a decision to make when it comes to how you react to the adverse weather conditions you're now facing.

Let's take a look at the bigger picture (assuming the weather isn't SO bad that the wedding has to be completely cancelled). This is mainly calling upon what we learnt about gratitude in Chapter 1.

- You are still getting married
- You still have someone in your life that you want to marry
- You still have the chance to spend time with people you've not seen for years and to celebrate a significant day in your life with them all
- You still have all the food
- You still have all the drinks
- Likely you still have all of the entertainment (though lawn games might be off if the lawn is now a swimming pool)

Need I go on?

This begs the question: what have you lost?

- You have lost the ability for you and your guests to spend an extended amount of time outside

- You might well have lost your outdoor photos and, whilst you might struggle to get quite as many perfect shots, you haven't lost them entirely

Obstacles can always be seen as opportunities. The rain pouring down on your wedding day is, with the right mindset, definitely an opportunity. For example, some of the most fun, interesting and creative wedding photographs have been taken in horrendous weather conditions – brides in wellies jumping in puddles; couples embracing the downpour, sheltered by a single umbrella; the bride and groom laughing as they run through the rain and thunder across the back lawn of the country house . . . I've seen so many great photos that have really captured the wonderful personalities of a couple, due to their ability to embrace the day *in spite* of the weather.

> SIDE NOTE: This is again where booking a top-rate wedding photographer will pay you back many times over. If the prospect of bad weather is a genuine concern for you, then take some time to discuss your "Plan B" with your photographer; if they're any good, they'll have back-up plans so good they'll seem like a "Plan A".

Let's look at some more examples of where obstacles can become opportunities, starting with one I often perhaps cause myself . . .

When your wedding supplier is already booked

When it comes to popular wedding dates, such as Saturdays in the summer months, professional wedding suppliers can be inundated with enquiries (one year I had 12 enquiries for a single date). For me, this means that I have to let down all but one or two couples, who have often contacted me saying that they specifically want to book me rather than just a magician. Until my cloning machine is operational, there's no immediate solution here.

There are two things which you can learn from this:

1. If you want a specific wedding supplier for your day, make sure that you contact them as early as possible. There's no advantage to waiting, even if your wedding date is a few years off.

2. Obstacles are opportunities. Missing out on a particular supplier forces you into a change – there's simply no point in wasting any time or energy complaining about the fact that you missed out, or assigning any blame. Get straight on with finding a solution and how you're going to use that solution to your advantage.
Consider these possibilities:

    - On reflection, you were going to be booking this particular type of supplier because you felt

like you *should*. Now that you can't book them, you might realise you don't *need* them, in which case you can save the money or spend it on something else
- Missing out on this supplier means that, in your search for a replacement, you find someone who is even better suited for your wedding
- The situation forces you to think about why you feel you need that supplier; now you can't book them, the time spent thinking about it actually causes a better idea to pop into your head

Any of these outcomes potentially presents a preferable solution; therefore view this situation as the opportunity that it is.

The extra-expensive wedding supplier

What if your dream supplier, whom you desperately want at your wedding, turns out to be twice as expensive as you'd envisaged? For some people, a supplier coming in at double the price is simply a mild inconvenience. For anyone on a tighter budget, this situation can of course present a problem.

You might be asking yourself how having to spend more money can be viewed as an opportunity – surely it is only an annoyance? Let's assume that not having this particular supplier is not negotiable – they absolutely HAVE to be a part of the wedding. (I've heard of couples changing their wedding dates so they can book certain photographers!)

Let's imagine a particular supplier. Let's call him Chris and picture him as a handsome, first-class magician. You've heard so much about him that he just has to be at your wedding. You're going to have to find a way to pay his fee.

Now, if you have a restricted budget, that money is of course going to have to be taken away from another area of the wedding set-up. And this is definitely an opportunity. Having a restriction like this will give you laser focus on the remaining things that you want to arrange. It will really cause you to question which of the remaining things you really NEED (remember the want/need section in Chapter 3). This may lead to certain things, which you had considered to be necessities, now being omitted from the day altogether. Or it might force you to embark on a DIY project, for example creating handmade centrepieces, which not only saves you the required money but also leads to a great night in with friends.

You've been dealt a hand of cards. Do you now proceed to bitch about the cards you've been dealt, or just enjoy playing the game?

The pressure of the wedding day

Everyone talks about a wedding being the best and/or the most important day of their life and any number of other superlative attributes. All this serves to invite an inordinate amount of pressure on the person/people organising the day itself, especially on you and your partner.

In truth, it is just another day. It has 24 hours in it, you'll wake up at the start of it and go to sleep at the end of it (and yes, I know it's not quite as simple as that, but bear with me).

Telling yourself that a certain thing absolutely has to be a certain way puts an immense amount of pressure on it. This not only makes it harder to enjoy in a relaxed and happy way, it also suggests that nothing is "allowed" to go wrong, because obviously if something did go wrong, then it wouldn't be the certain way it HAS to be. Let's consider an example that is incredibly easy to equate to your wedding day.

The best nights out

We've all experienced this – suddenly and somehow the stars align and fate conspires to give you and all your best friends the chance to have a night out together. You then spend ages planning what you're going to do, what you're going to wear, where best to go for a pre-evening drink, the ideal main venue, and everything else that is guaranteed to be the best night out you'll ever have. The big night comes and everything seems to go to plan but, for what seems like no apparent reason, it all suddenly feels a bit of an anti-climax. That is almost certainly due the pressure that all of you have placed on the night being a success, which has strangled the spontaneity and fun out of the event, making it instead all feel a bit forced.

You must also have experienced the following . . .

A couple of your friends have decided to pop down to the local pub; you're not really sure if you're up for it but drag yourself out, telling your partner you'll be back within two hours. When you arrive, the pub seems livelier than normal, someone you haven't seen for a year appears, there's a great little band playing and you find yourself sneaking away, only to text your partner that you'll be home later than you'd thought.

Before you know it, it's 3 am and you're at a night club ten miles away . . . and this becomes "that night" that you and your friends will laugh about for years. There had been no pressure on you to do or be anything different from normal, and no pressure to make the night brilliant. You just had a good time.

How do we transition this into your wedding day, though? It's not like you can turn up without a care in the world, wearing jeggings and your favourite old sweatshirt, is it? Well, this is where the reserve clause comes in.

Reserve clause

It's likely that you have at some point failed, because of some uncalled-for intervention, at something that should have been simple. Or, the exact opposite, you've succeeded when failing would have felt so much easier. Either of those situations will help you to understand the power and necessity of a reserve clause when it comes to remaining realistic about life and removing pressure from situations.

Sod's Law (aka Murphy's Law) states that anything that can go wrong will go wrong. We've probably all felt this to be true at various times in our lives.

What if we accounted for Sod's Law in anything that we promised ourselves, by building in a reserve clause? This would change "My wedding day is going to be the best day of my life" into the entirely less pressured "My wedding day is going to be the best day of my life, providing that nothing happens to prevent it from being so". That is admittedly quite a lot more of a mouthful, but it's more of a mental practice than something you're going to drop casually into conversation.

The reserve clause isn't a difficult concept to explain or understand, but adopting it allows you to release a lot of pressure and thus be much truer and kinder to yourself. Combining this concept with the skills already covered, of being grateful and understanding control, will put you mentally into a powerful position when immersing yourself in your wedding planning, allowing you to fully enjoy being present during the whole day.

Conclusion on amor fati

The Stoics have taught us that it is not what happens to us that defines how we feel, but how we decide to react to our circumstances that determines our levels of enjoyment and satisfaction. Whatever happens will happen. After anything has happened, there is no chance to go back and do things differently. Expending energy wishing things were different is, quite literally, wasted energy.

The only life you're able to live is the one you are in now, and the only circumstances you have are the ones that this life has presented to you. Embracing whatever happens around you is a trait of someone who is truly present and centred; it places you in the very best situation possible to react to whatever life, fate and/or the gods throw at you, without your tranquillity being disturbed.

> "Endurance is not just the ability to bear
> a hard thing, but to turn it into glory."
>
> William Barclay

Being a Stoic Bride will empower you to:

- Love fate and accept the circumstances that it delivers
- Recognise obstacles as opportunities and make the most out of them

- Understand that any situation you are in is the ONLY situation you're in, and allow you to respond accordingly

- Understand that sacrificing your tranquillity due to an unhelpful situation will get you nowhere

- Use the reserve clause to remove the pressure of everything going right

CHAPTER 6
Being the gatekeeper

Each of us has our own "gatekeeper" in our brain. This is called our "critical faculty", through which all information we receive has to pass. Our critical faculty can be thought of as a filter, which compares the information we already know and hold true with any new information we receive. We don't have to think about doing it – our brains just automatically check new information against our previous experiences.

If someone starts shouting about peas not being green, then our critical faculty checks this against what we know to be true and says "Er, yes they are". There is absolutely no doubt in our brains that peas are green.

This is an incredibly useful function for our brains – when we encounter a situation or event we have encountered before, we automatically know what we need to do. For example: "Ah, look – a door – I know what these do", and "Oh, look – a tiger – run!". If we approached a door and every time had to try to interpret what it was and how we had to make it open or close, then we'd all be pretty inefficient creatures. Similarly, we wouldn't last for very long if we tried to hug big, stripy cats because they look pretty.

The downside to the critical faculty is that we can often have a false-belief system "installed" into our brains, typically because of something happening to us, which has caused us to learn incorrectly from it. Our critical faculty can then end up making decisions that are based on belief rather than fact, which can lead to unrealistic fears and anxieties.

For example: Incident A occurred when you were a child, where a goose ran at you, causing you to fall over and graze your knee. Your brain has thereby learnt that geese are very dangerous and can hurt you easily, and that you mustn't go within 100 metres of them. Whenever you later encounter a goose, your brain looks for similar incidents in your memory and finds Incident A. You then cannot help but respond as if you are faced with a very real threat.

We also have another part of our brains, the prefrontal cortex, which controls our cognitive behaviour, decision making, personality and expression, and moderates social behaviour (you won't be surprised to hear that drinking alcohol can have a moderate to severe impact on reducing the function of the prefrontal cortex!). The biggest difference between this part of the brain and the critical faculty is that what happens in the prefrontal cortex is controlled primarily by conscious brain activity – we do, at least to a certain extent, have awareness and control over it.

The purpose of this chapter is to teach you techniques to make you consciously able to be your own gatekeeper, allowing you to decide what information you will give permission to come in and join the party in your head and which bits of information are definitely NOT on the guest list (and certainly can't come in wearing *those* shoes).

Permission (yes, again)

This is slightly different from the concept of permission we covered earlier. In Chapter 4 we talked about you giving yourself permission to trust your decisions and to decide how other people's opinions affect you. Now we are talking about you giving yourself permission to decide how external *events* affect you.

It'd be great if you could simply decide not to give permission for anything to affect you, but hey – you're human. Experiencing emotion is important – it's fundamentally what makes us human. It can therefore feel difficult simply to decide that you're not going to let an event affect you, but this honestly doesn't have to be difficult at all – please consider this as a skill that you can learn and improve with practice. There are numerous techniques that you can employ in order to improve your skills. You can think of each of these techniques as a tool from a toolkit – you simply select the appropriate tool, depending upon the task at hand. If you wanted to knock a nail into a wall, you'd use your hammer not your hacksaw, right? Similarly, different mental tools will work differently for different people and for different circumstances.

Only you can find out and decide – through repetition and trial and error – which tools work best for you. The only effort I've made to segregate these techniques is to split them into two sections: "in-the-moment techniques" and "longer-term techniques". This doesn't mean you can't use an in-the-moment technique for a longer-term situation – you need to do whatever works best for you.

Generally speaking, though, in-the-moment techniques are for when you experience an external event that is trying to perturb you right here, right now. You may have overheard a negative comment at your wedding, or maybe your partner has once again left their work clothes *next to* rather than *in* the washing basket. Longer-term techniques are generally better suited for ongoing issues, for things that have happened in the past, or for things that are going to happen in the future, which you're allowing to affect your tranquillity.

In-the-moment techniques

Here are three exercises designed to help you learn how best to cope with any negative emotions caused by an external event. The techniques of course won't provide any immediate solution to the event itself, but they will help you to feel calmer, more confident and more able to cope with the situation.

EXERCISE 9
DEEP BREATHING

You know this already. You've been told this by tens of people before in various different situations. The reason you've heard it so many times is because it works!

Now, you can just take a deep breath and let it go, then repeat a few times, which will undoubtedly have some effect. But I prefer and recommend a technique called the "4, 7, 8 technique".

It's incredibly simple:

1. Breathe in through your nose for the count of 4
2. Hold your breath for a count of 7
3. Breathe out of your mouth for the count of 8
4. Repeat three or four times, or until you feel you've calmed down

From a physiological point of view, this method of deep breathing has multiple benefits:

- It brings more oxygen into the body. This allows your heart rate to slow, your muscles to relax and your blood pressure to lower, all of which reduce the levels of stress in your body and mind

- It gives you the ability to focus easily on something that isn't the source of your anxiety. You probably already appreciate that trying *not* to think about something only makes you think even more about it. But stopping for a few minutes and focusing on regulating your breathing, while enjoying the feelings of reduced stress, will enable you to stop thinking about other things

- It demonstrates that you are in that moment fully in control of the thing you are focusing on, i.e. your breath. This can give a vitally relaxing and grounding effect if or when you feel as if everything is out of your control

- Finally, it gives you some positive time out, enabling you to compose your thoughts and mentally distance yourself from whatever has perturbed you

It takes less than two minutes to run five times through the five steps of the 4, 7, 8 technique. That very short period of time really can make a significant difference to how you're feeling. However stressed and pressed for time you are feeling, I urge you to find just two minutes to help yourself feel better. You don't even need to close your eyes or find a quiet spot – you can do this technique in just about any situation.

The 4, 7, 8 technique is a great way to deal with in-the-moment situations such as anger, stress and anxiety, but there's nothing to stop you using this technique on a regular basis, to free up your mind and feel better and more in control. I hope you will allow yourself to get used to practising the technique as often as you can, to start enjoying all the physiological and emotional benefits.

EXERCISE 10
THE NEXT-ONE-SECOND TECHNIQUE

I love this technique and have shared it with many people who have sought my help within a therapy situation on a wide range of issues, as well as with friends and new acquaintances. I can't remember where I first heard of this technique or started using it, but I know that I'm definitely not the person who created it, as much as I would like to be. It is a great technique to use when you're feeling overwhelmed by something; as someone who has suffered with various issues in the past, this has been utterly invaluable to me at times.

The basis of the technique is to set yourself a micro-goal, achieve the goal, acknowledge your success, and repeat.

Let's consider an example, to illustrate the process. I make no apologies for the subject matter here – IBS is a potentially embarrassing and debilitating condition, which is suffered by an estimated 10–20% of the UK population, and can cause a wide range of unpleasant symptoms, including cramping, abdominal pain, bloating, gas, diarrhoea and constipation.

Many people remain blissfully unaware of the difficulties, even those experienced by friends they know who suffer from IBS, but the anxiety and physical tension it causes can have a highly detrimental effect on a sufferer's day-to-day life. I'm going to ask you now to imagine how this might affect you on your wedding day. This will obviously be easier for anyone who does suffer from IBS; if you don't, please take the time to empathise with anyone who does by picturing yourself in this situation.

Your IBS frequently causes you anxiety about where the nearest toilet is and whether you'll be able to make it there in time. Thanks to extensive medical tests, and to the strict diet you scrupulously follow, you know that there is nothing physical that might cause a flare-up on your wedding day. However, your symptoms are exacerbated at times when you are under stress or anxiety.

Right now, you are about to walk down the aisle to join your partner, in front of all your family and friends. You've been mentally preparing yourself to feel calm on your wedding day, including deep breathing on the way to the ceremony, but the very fact that you *might* need to dash to the loo is making this moment feel unavoidably stressful. As you stand outside the church, your stomach starts cramping and every part of your being is telling you to run to the nearest loo. Your brain starts to make you panic about where the toilet is, the fact that you can't just slip your dress off easily, and whether you'll even can last through the ceremony without having an accident.

The next-one-second technique starts with a question, which you now ask yourself, each time answering with 'Yes':

1. Can I get through the next one second? Yes

2. By the time you've had a chance to answer this, you've already made it through that one second – congratulate yourself

3. Can I make it through the next three seconds? Yes

4. Count to three – congratulate yourself

5. Can I make it through five seconds? Yes

6. Count to five – congratulate yourself

7. You've now made it through nine seconds – well done

8. Can I make it through 10 seconds? Yes

9. Count to 10 – congratulate yourself

10. Repeat this, increasing the length of time each time, until you feel ready to set yourself the goal of getting through the total amount of time you need to get through

With this specific example, you would need to reach at least half an hour in total. That goal might seem unattainable while you are standing there outside the church and imagining all eyes on you as you walk in. But what's excellent about this technique is the ability to start it all over again – you could work up to just 15 minutes to start with. Once you've reached the 15 minutes, you can then go back to the goal of getting through just the next second and run through the process again. This can be done in the background of your mind rather than you having to fully focus on it, and you will find it easier and easier the more times you practise it.

In the run-up to your wedding, practise this whole process in any slightly stressful situation, to make you even stronger when it comes to your big day.

The anticipation of a potentially stressful event is always, always, *always* worse than when you are actually there, in the moment. Without wanting to sound too clichéd, once you see the smiling and supportive faces of your family and friends, you'll find that it really is possible to allow your worries to fade away.

At the points in this exercise when I say to congratulate yourself, I really mean that you should do this. Not with the faintest trace of irony, sarcastically slow-clapping to yourself while saying, "Oh well done, you survived, like, a few seconds". You need to do something internally which would make you feel as if you've done something well – a real and actual commendation to yourself for what you've achieved. Giving yourself a silent "Well done" or a hand squeeze can be incredibly effective in increasing your confidence and sense of achievement.

You might be thinking, "But Chris, I only went one second without running to the toilet – big deal". Sure, that might not feel like a big deal to other people, but success is relative. Everyone has their problems, their fears, their anxieties and their foibles. Your issue is your issue; it is 100% fine, and nobody else in the room will have the slightest clue that you are congratulating yourself for what you have achieved.

This technique works particularly well because success breeds success – when people achieve something, they tend to feel better about themselves and thus feel they can go on to achieve more. Achieving micro-goals one by one is the perfect way to take advantage of this. It doesn't matter how small each achievement is, it will empower you to reach a slightly larger one.

EXERCISE 11
THOUGHT STOPPING

This is another of my favourite techniques, straight from the therapy room. It is powerful, deliberately jarring and actually quite fun. It is once again a skill to be learnt through practice, so initial success doesn't define how well it will work for you on a long-term basis. You *will* get better and better at this the more you do it.

We'll start with some questions:

- Is anxiety an issue for you?
- Does your brain tend to overthink things?
- Do you worry about circumstances that you know just won't happen?
- Have you ever started to worry about something that is so far in the future that you were probably the first person even to consider it?
- Do you create situations to worry about?
- Do you often ponder the worst-case scenario?

If you've answered yes to any of these questions, then "thought stopping" could well be your new best friend.

At the beginning of this book, I gave a brief overview of the history of Stoicism, and touched on the fact that a lot of Stoicism is based around logic and truth. Whilst "truth" and "logic" aren't dictionary opposites of "worry" and "anxiety", they're certainly not at all similar to those words.

Can you think of a time when you've been unreasonably worried about a situation in which you were thinking entirely logically and truthfully?

It's okay, I'll wait. (I'm not judging at all!)

To gain full understanding of this exercise, we need to go into a bit more detail about thoughts and what we're "allowed" to think about. Now, clearly we're allowed to think about whatever we choose – there's no thought police (yet!). However, it is most helpful for us only to "allow" thoughts that are empowering or helpful to us. That means that any thoughts that are untrue, unhelpful or negative should be discarded instantly.

But how can we do this?

In this exercise, we need to practise noticing our thoughts and policing them very strictly. I will go into more detail below about which thoughts aren't allowed, but let's first cover the technique itself.

How to thought stop:

1. Focus on something you're worried or anxious about
2. Notice what you're thinking about it
3. Check in to see if your thought is "allowed"

4. Interrupt the thought by shouting "STOP!" at yourself, or jarring yourself in some other way, before interjecting with logic to prove to yourself that what you are worrying about is not a cause for worry or anxiety

In my therapy room, while clients were talking me through their stream of consciousness relating to an issue, the moment they included "not-allowed thoughts", I'd clap my hands together as loudly as I could and firmly say "STOP!". This jolt serves as a strong reminder to the brain that it shouldn't work in this way.

I would explain why I had interjected, why a particular thought was unhelpful, and what a more helpful and logical thought would be. If you're in public, clearly you don't have to shout out loud – there are other thought-stopping actions you can take to startle your brain, such as clicking your fingers, or simply imagining a huge "STOP!" sign suddenly appearing in front of you.

The only tricky part in this otherwise simple exercise is catching the thoughts as quickly as possible. I will describe some potential real-life examples after covering "not-allowed thoughts".

Thoughts that are not allowed

1. Catastrophising
   Do you ever find yourself imagining the worst-case scenario, for example your wedding venue catching

fire, your dress splitting in half as you walk down the aisle, or your partner breaking his leg on the dance floor? If you do ever anticipate something disastrous happening in a situation, and then find yourself believing the worst and worrying about that disaster actually happening, then you are catastrophising.

Catastrophic thinking is wholly unhelpful – you have no idea what will happen in the future and, unless you are having these thoughts with the specific goal of preparing yourself for the worst-case scenario (as in the negative visualisation exercise in Chapter 1), then you are only causing yourself unnecessary anxiety and worry.

If you are catastrophising, STOP!

2. Mind reading

   No, this isn't the Derren Brown part of my job. In this context, I mean whenever you *assume* that you know what someone is thinking about you, your wedding, your life, etc, etc. If you DO actually know 100% what someone else is thinking, then a career on stage is calling! Otherwise, you are "mind reading", which can be incredibly damaging both to you and to the other person.

   If you are mind reading, STOP!

3. Negative filtering (aka "ignoring the positive")

   We've all done this. For example: you're in a bad

mood after a trying day at work and you go home and tell your partner about everything. You report on everything that is even 1% negative but neglect to mention any of the positive things that happened. Even if you are normally quite positive, your low mood and/or damaged self-esteem somehow prevent you from seeing the bright side to anything at that moment.

If you're filtering the negative, STOP!

4. All-or-nothing thinking

    Nothing complicated here – this is about believing a situation is black or white, as if there is no middle ground or any grey area. It has to be all or nothing. Examples of this in your wedding planning might include "If we don't get that venue, the wedding's going to be rubbish", "If I don't wear that £3,000 dress, I'm going to look terrible", or "If Chris Piercy isn't available, we might as well not bother with any entertainment". Life is very rarely binary and thinking that it is can be very unhelpful.

    If you're engaging in all-or-nothing thinking, STOP!

5. Fact or opinion?

    If someone says something that upsets you, take a quick step back and look at whether what they have said is a fact or an opinion. If someone has provided an opinion, then it is worth exactly what you paid for it: nothing. So, whilst they're entitled

to tell you something, that doesn't make their opinion a fact. If there is truth to their opinion, then this needs to be processed as the other types of thoughts above.
If a negative thought you're experiencing is based only on someone else's opinion, STOP!

6. Overgeneralising/labelling
   Is what you're thinking a blanket statement based on an isolated event? For example, if you become aware that one person has said you have bad taste in clothes, do you go on to believe that everyone must be thinking or saying the same? Not only is that one statement that you heard only an opinion, but your conclusion is a massive overgeneralisation. If you're overgeneralising, STOP!

Example scenarios of thought stopping

Example 1 – At your wedding, someone knocks over the wedding cake, and your brain starts off into overdrive about how the day is ruined.

STOP!

The day is not ruined – one bad thing has happened. You are overgeneralising; one bad thing happening does not mean the rest of the day is ruined. The cake situation will be resolved, and the day will continue.

Example 2 – You're panicking the day before the wedding about everything going completely wrong.

STOP!

You are catastrophising. You cannot predict the future and have no proof at all that anything will go wrong. You have done everything you can; now you must love and embrace whatever does happen (amor fati).

Example 3 – You show the bridesmaids their dresses, one of them makes a comment about not liking the colour, so you start thinking about how the dresses are going to have to be changed.

STOP!

If one of your bridesmaids has complained about the colour, is this a fact or only her opinion? It's an opinion, to which she is entitled. You are also negative filtering – what positive things have the bridesmaids said to you about the dresses? Before you make any decision to change anything, make sure you include ALL opinions, positive and negative, and giving priority to your own. Remember, this is your day – we're talking dictatorship here, not democracy.

I hope that you now have a clear understanding of thought stopping and how incredibly helpful it can be in reducing (and STOPPING!) unhelpful thoughts. Now you only have to practise the technique as often as you can, in order to start naturally blocking all unnecessary worries and anxiety from your mind.

EXERCISE 12
REMEMBERING YOUR SPHERE OF INFLUENCE

This is a simple exercise for you, to finish off the in-the-moment techniques.

Whenever something unfortunate happens or you're worrying about something, take a step back and look at whether you actually have any control over the situation at all. Is what's happening within your sphere of influence? If yes, then do what you can about it. If not, then let it go – there's nothing you can do anyway.

Long-term techniques

Whilst some of the techniques below can also be used in the moment, they are usually especially helpful in allowing you to overcome long-term issues and/or to prepare in advance for specific circumstances and events that may disturb your tranquillity.

EXERCISE 13
THE BEST-FRIEND TECHNIQUE

I used to love using this in therapy sessions and I can't explain how much you're going to love it too. If you've ever wanted to say something that feels like an utter "mic drop" moment, then this is it. You're welcome!

We've all got that friend who is constantly putting him- or herself down, right? They'll go off on a monologue about how they're this or they're that or they're ugly or they're fat or they're blah blah blah. If you don't have a friend like that, then maybe you are that person (awkward!). But I don't say that to be insensitive – I am all too aware that we all have our insecurities. It's natural to enjoy being reassured about anything, and saying horrible things about ourselves is a sure-fire way to gain encouraging reassurance from others.

Try this on someone the next time they start putting themselves down, and then you can later start applying it to yourself. When you notice someone saying something horrible about themselves, stop and ask them the following:

"Would you say that about your best friend?"

"Oh god, no."

"Why not?"

"It's an awful thing to say to someone. They would be really hurt if they heard me say that."

"Then why are you saying it about yourself?"

#MICDROP

CHAPTER 6 – BEING THE GATEKEEPER

I'm sure you can imagine people's faces as they search for reasons, excuses and explanations to justify why they think it is okay to talk about themselves as if they're a piece of rubbish, but that it's 100% inappropriate to say *exactly* the same thing about a friend.

This is an example of the insane levels of double-standards that we impose on ourselves, typically without even realising we're doing it, and also without recognising how damaging we are being to ourselves.

Be honest with yourself – how many times have you told yourself you are stupid or ugly, boring or useless, too fat or too skinny? Now compare that with the number of times you've said the same to a friend. How many times have you looked at yourself in a new outfit, thought you looked awful and told yourself exactly that. Now compare this again with how many times you've told a best friend that they look terrible in what they're wearing. How many times have you told yourself you're stupid, you're crazy or you're a horrible person? Again, how many times have you said those sorts of things to your best friend?

Now, unless you're already incredibly well-centred, or you act with sociopathic levels of honesty, I reckon that the difference between how many times you say negative things to yourself is going to be vastly higher than how often you criticise your friends. But why? Why do we do this? Why do we allow this?

You're a human being with feelings, as are your friends – if you believe in equality, what gives you the right to treat two humans differently just because one of them happens to be you? If you have what you believe to be a solid answer to this question, then I would genuinely love you to send it to me – info@chrispiercymagic.co.uk.

I'm going to ask you to start employing the best-friend technique from this moment forward, for the rest of your life. It is incredibly simple and takes hardly any practice, apart from getting into the habit of noticing whenever you say anything mean to yourself, passing unkind judgment, which you would simply never do to a friend (or anyone else, for that matter). From this moment forward, I want you to treat yourself as you would treat your best friend.

It goes something like this . . .

Amira's brain: "Amira, look at yourself. How can you even contemplate going out looking like that? You're fat, you look awful in that outfit, and your hair looks like you had a fight with the cat. What a munter."

Amira: "Hold on a minute, darling brain . . . would you say all those horrible things to James?"

Amira's brain: "No – we love James. He would hate us – and himself – if we said anything like that to him."

Amira: "Oh, really?"

Amira's brain: "Of course!"

Amira: "Why are you saying those things to me, then?"

Amira's brain struggles with answer

Amira: "Brain, shut the hell up."

This technique is about as simple as it gets. You just have to make sure you aren't an absolute bitch to yourself. Be kind to yourself, always.

The humanist psychologist, Carl Rogers, who developed much of the modern-day thinking of psychology, put this in a way that I think is just beautiful. He says we should treat people with "unconditional positive regard", and that this also extends to how we treat ourselves.

I'm not suggesting that you're instantly going to be able to remember to pull yourself up on every crappy comment or thought you have about yourself. But let's say you had 100 unhelpful thoughts about yourself in a day – from tiny self-doubts to damning judgments – NONE of them would be doing you any good, and every single one is at least a bit damaging. Even if you caught only 20% of them on the first day, that would leave you with a significant reduction, at only 80 critical thoughts that day. Then, as you get used to employing the best-friend technique, you'll catch more and more of the negativity. And before too long, you'll even find yourself stopping to tell your new best friend something really kind and positive. Imagine how powerful it could be if we learnt to compliment ourselves as much as we used to belittle ourselves – take a moment to think about that.

Mindfulness

Mindfulness has gained in popularity in the last few years, and this can only be considered a good thing. Whoever you are and whatever you do, having the ability to be mindful is an invaluable skill. There have been countless books written on the topic of mindfulness alone; if what I write in this book piques your interest, I strongly recommend that you read further on the subject to gain a fuller understanding.

Mindfulness can be practised daily for the relief of just about any type of stress or anxiety. The techniques can also be used in the moment. I tend to use mindfulness if I am having trouble sleeping – you know, those annoying nights when your brain simply won't turn off? For me, that's when mindfulness comes into its own. But it can be used in just about any situation, to allow you to take a step back, reappraise your situation, and realise just how little you need to be worrying about in that moment.

But what is mindfulness?

In short, mindfulness is a psychological process in which you learn to focus your attention on things that are happening in the present moment. The next step is to allow whatever you're experiencing just to happen, without passing any judgment – you simply let things be as they are. There are various methods to achieve this, but I'm going to describe my own method. This isn't an entirely original and unique method, but an amalgamation of the techniques that I have found have worked best for me. You'll be pleased to know that there really isn't anything complicated whatsoever about this.

EXERCISE 14 – MINDFULNESS MEDITATION TECHNIQUE

You might be happy to keep your eyes closed, as suggested below, for this exercise. However, please don't feel you have to if that is difficult or uncomfortable in any way – you will still gain from the exercise if you follow it with your eyes open.

If you are happy to shut your eyes, you can simply read through the whole exercise a couple of times before starting, to memorise the steps (don't worry – the steps are logical and easy to remember). Or, if or when you are somewhere you can listen in peace to an audio recording, go to www.chrispiercymagic.co.uk/bwp-exercises to hear my extended explanation and recording of this exercise, which will be even easier to follow and more effective.

1. Find somewhere you can feel comfortable closing your eyes for an extended period
2. Sit or lie down and make yourself comfortable

3. Close your eyes and begin to concentrate on your breathing
4. Notice any small changes you feel in your body as you breathe in and out
5. Now just begin to notice whatever you notice
6. Whatever you notice, tell yourself that thing is okay, and move on, allowing your mind to move onto anything else it chooses
7. Repeat steps 5 and 6

You might be looking for a bit more clarity on "notice whatever you notice", in point 5; it really couldn't be much simpler. Here's an example of a typical "conversation" that might occur in my head when I'm using mindfulness to help me get to sleep:

"I'm noticing the duvet resting on my big toe, and that's okay. I'm noticing a thought about the *Game of Thrones* episode I just watched, and that's okay. I'm noticing how my breath fills my chest when I inhale, and that's okay. I'm noticing how the bed beneath me feels, and that's okay." And so on.

Whatever it is that you notice, just tell yourself that it's okay; if you notice it again, tell yourself that it's okay again.

If for any reason this feels uncomfortable or pointless to you, compare it with the following approach, which is a train of thoughts more likely to run through your mind while you're lying in bed, feeling frustrated about not falling asleep:

"Why does the duvet always feel so heavy? Right, I'll move my foot – that's better – but oh, man, now my leg feels in the wrong position. I'll move the duvet. Argh, now my top half isn't as warm. I wonder how *Game of Thrones* will end, I reckon that if . . . blah . . . blah . . . blah."

And suddenly, it's 3 am and you're still awake.

This exercise isn't only for getting to sleep. There will be plenty of times in your day-to-day life when you feel frustrated, fed up, overwhelmed and/or stressed by the millions of things buzzing round in your head. And, especially with wedding planning being uncharted territory and with the numerous associated pressures, it's likely you will experience that state of mental turmoil more often than normal.

Whenever you are in that situation, find time as soon as you can to relax by yourself and complete this exercise. If you only have five minutes, you will still return feeling refreshed and recentred. If you have a little longer, you could treat yourself to a free mindfulness guided meditation on YouTube. Either way, you will have used this brief introduction to mindfulness to help you to feel more in control of all the thoughts buzzing around in your brain.

Mental preparation

This has some crossover with the technique of negative visualisation covered in Chapter 1. In the negative visualisation exercise, you were asked to imagine things going as badly as possible in order to create a feeling of gratitude for the things that you have in your life and your wedding. Whilst we are going to be using visualisation again, this is with a more specific and targeted approach. If there is a scenario within your life or your wedding that makes you feel particularly uncomfortable, this mental-preparation exercise could be invaluable.

**EXERCISE 15
COPING TO MASTERY EXERCISE**

You might be happy to keep your eyes closed, as suggested below, for most of this exercise. However, please don't feel you have to if that is difficult or uncomfortable in any way – you will still gain from the exercise if you follow it with your eyes open.

If you are happy to shut your eyes, you can simply read through the whole exercise a couple of times before starting, to memorise the steps (don't worry – the steps are logical and easy to remember). Or, if or when you are somewhere you can listen in peace to an audio recording, go to www.chrispiercymagic.co.uk/bwp-exercises to hear my extended explanation and recording of this exercise, which will be even easier to follow and more effective.

1. Think of a scenario in which you'd like to feel more comfortable

2. Give yourself a score, from 1 to 10, on how confident you'd feel in the scenario, where 1 signifies no confidence and 10 means it'll be a breeze

3. Find somewhere comfortable where you're not going to be disturbed and close your eyes

4. Spend a minute or so concentrating on your breathing and becoming relaxed

5. Now begin to imagine yourself into the scenario. You can imagine it almost as a film clip, which you can play, pause and stop, and the clip has an end when the scenario has been completed

6. Imagine going through that scenario from start to finish in your mind, taking time to truly visualise and sense every aspect. Imagine the colours, the shapes, the people, the setting, your feelings, the ambience, the sounds, the smells, the tastes – everything that might engage your senses in the scenario you're thinking of

7. Once you've been through the scenario, give yourself a score out of 10 for how confident you felt doing it

8. Imagine yourself now filling up with more confidence. Take a deep breath and imagine that you're actually able to inhale confidence itself and allow it to spread throughout your body. Then exhale the breath, leaving the confidence inside you

9. Now imagine going through that scenario again but with this new sense of confidence about you – imagine it in all the amazing detail you created before

10. Once again, give yourself a score out of 10 for your confidence level. Hopefully it will have increased, even if it is just by one point. Then repeat steps 6, 7 and 8 until you feel your confidence for that scenario is at a 10

But how will all this help? We're going to go back to the rollercoaster – which *isn't* like life itself – to gain a better understanding.

Imagine now that you're on a rollercoaster. You've never been on one before, so have no idea what to expect. Now you're finding yourself thrown around left and right, twisting in all directions, faster and faster, upside down, corkscrewing around – it's possibly the most alarming thing you've ever experienced.

Now think about how your experience would be if you got straight back on that rollercoaster again. Exactly the same twists, turns and loops, but this time you would at least have some anticipation of what was coming, which would inevitably make you feel at least a little more prepared and less alarmed, even if the ride was still a bit scary.

What if you went on for a third time, a fourth time . . . a tenth time? Be honest – do you really believe you could ever feel as scared, as exhilarated, as shaken up, on your tenth (or twentieth) time as you did on your first? I don't think you could. By this stage, you'd know the route like the back of your hand and you'd know that it would all end safely, so nothing would feel as shocking or terrifying.

Mentally visualising a scenario might not be quite as effective as physically experiencing the situation in real life, but I think you will be astonished by the effectiveness of this coping to mastery exercise. After all, your thoughts and memories of a situation are purely in your mind – if you have taken time to visualise and run through a scenario as clearly as you can, you will have trained your brain to become used to everything that is likely to happen in that scenario, nearly as effectively as if you had actually experienced it in real life.

Conclusion on being the gatekeeper

Unhelpful things will happen in your life.

People will say horrible stuff.

People will do awful things.

While all these things are true and inescapable, the only important thing is how you allow them to affect you. By standing vigilantly at the gate of your mind, you can decide what you are going to let in, what you are going to discard, and what you are going to do with anything that you allow through the gates.

This chapter has given you a host of techniques for dealing with a variety of situations. If you diligently keep those techniques at your mind's gate, you will move into a more commanding situation in your life.

Being a Stoic Bride will empower you to:

- Understand that you have control over what you allow to affect you

- Use various techniques to keep yourself tranquil

- Treat yourself as you would your best friend

- Treat yourself with unconditional positive regard

- Pre-empt stressful situations and prepare your mind to feel less stressed about them

CHAPTER 7
Remembering we're all human

In the opening pages of this book, I went into some detail about what Stoicism is and what it is not. Despite me telling you categorically that it is not the same as "being stoic" about something and not showing any emotion at all, it might be that you are beginning to feel that's what it actually is.

Yes, I'm asking you to not worry about things you can't control.

Yes, I'm asking you to be grateful for the important things in your life.

Yes, I'm asking you to remember that even finding someone to love and to love you back is a triumph in itself.

Yes, I'm asking you to learn to restrict your emotional responses to situations.

BUT . . .

I'm not asking you to forget that you are, and we all are, human beings.

Being a human means that, whatever happens, we still have choices, we still have feelings, we still have emotions and, perhaps most importantly, we are very capable of making mistakes (and bloody big mistakes, at that!).

Complex emotional feelings are largely what distinguish us from other creatures on this planet and also stop us from acting like robots. People who do not show any emotion at all are thought of as cold and robotic (some might say Stoic, but we know that they are wrong about that!).

Emotions

Emotions are a communication device. At their base level, they allow us to understand our feelings, and to convey them to other people as well as ourselves.

Every single emotion is valid and every single emotion is also useful. It is actually vital for our own mental states to learn how to be comfortable with all our emotions – yes ALL of them – even the taboo ones like anger, jealousy and sadness.

We all already know that when something fairly significant happens, our body is going to check in on how we should respond to the situation and then generate an emotional response – that's human nature. Stoicism doesn't expect you or even ask you to be able to turn off a natural response; instead it asks you to accept the emotion, own it, let it pass and then to make whatever decisions need to be made in a logical and thoughtful way.

> "Stoicism is about the domestication of emotions, not their elimination."
>
> Nassim Nicholas Taleb

If you have any doubt about this, ask yourself this: how many great decisions have you made in your life when you've been at the height of emotion? I'm sure there have been the odd few good decisions in there but, in general, people make awful decisions (including for the long term) when they are feeling particularly emotional. That is why I'm going to suggest that you stop doing that and become more Stoical about your emotions.

Everything is okay!

There is a certain expectancy within modern society, in particular from social media, that everyone always has to look good, feel good and tell everyone how great their life is. The bottom line here: that type of expectancy completely sucks.

You might already be thinking about people you know who are generally unhappy with their lives, yet plaster their Instagram with smiling selfies, add statuses to Facebook about how great their life is, and have Snapchat stories that feel like a fairy tale when compared with the reality of their situation. This isn't really their fault – social peer pressure is, albeit it subconsciously, forcing people's hands into this world of fakery, in which it can feel more important to give the impression of a happy existence than to focus on living their real life. It can feel more important, for example, for people to see your gym selfie, than for you to put in the work at the gym and reap the benefits. And taking a photo of your meal to show everyone where you are and what you're eating can feel more important than fully appreciating the food and the restaurant.

What is driving this is ego, pure and simple. And ego is simply not your friend. For more on this, read *Ego is the Enemy* by Ryan Holiday.

Stepping back from what has turned into a bit of a rant about social media, and concentrating on real life – what if when we were happy, we made that obvious in our disposition to others? What if when we were sad, we told people we were sad? What if we told people when they had angered us, or when we were in pain (mental, physical or emotional) – would that be so bad?

I'm here to tell you that all your emotions are okay. Emotions are here for a reason. They help protect us, they help us make our decisions and they help us grow and thrive. Every single person on this planet experiences positive and negative emotions, so there is no reason to feel guilty about having any of them. BUT (you knew there was going to be a but) it is important that we are in control of our emotions and not the other way around.

The transience of emotions

Another significant part of Stoic philosophy is to remember that every single emotion and feeling is transient. By that, I mean that no feeling can last for ever, which includes the good, the bad and the ugly of emotions.

Emotions are not designed to sit within us for ever. Every emotion serves as a response to a stimulus, to communicate a need to react. We need to process that emotion, make our decision on how to react, and then move on.

Even the powerhouse emotion of grief doesn't give constant sadness, although that's sometimes how it can feel. When you lose someone you love, you will feel sad and then later you'll find yourself happily remembering a fond memory. Then you might feel guilty about the fact you were feeling happy. Then you'll feel angry at some higher power because that person is no longer alive, and then you'll feel sad again. Grief provides a very random and cyclical range of emotions.

Ever heard someone say, "Oh, I can't stay mad at him"? This is a very true statement – it is quite simply impossible to stay angry with someone, and why would you even want to? Sitting in the feeling of anger is pretty unpleasant, so why would you want to stay there? But this doesn't mean that anger shouldn't get processed just like all your other emotions, even when someone has wronged you so badly that you've made the decision to remove them from your life entirely. You don't stay angry at them for the rest of your life – you are wronged, you get angry, you then process the anger, cut the person from your life and, by doing so, the anger subsides whilst you carry on with your life. If or when you see that person again, then sure, that feeling of anger might resurface. But you haven't been angry at them that entire time. I'm hoping I'm making this distinction clear.

You might be familiar with the phrase "This too shall pass", which comments on the fleeting nature of situations and emotions. It can comfort the person who is suffering but also chasten the person who is succeeding.

Whatever emotion you are feeling, it WILL pass.

Owning your feelings

If this is the only thing you take on board from this section of the book, I will be very happy. It's potentially a life changer – I'm absolutely serious when I say that. Owning your feelings is pretty simple, really – you just accept that however you are feeling is okay, don't try and fight the feelings you are feeling, and take the emotions as they are. This is in general really easy to do with happiness, joy, confidence and other pleasant emotions, but people tend to find it harder with the ones we're "not supposed to have" such as sadness and anger.

Each and every emotion has its own role to play and a job to do. If you don't own that emotion when it arises, you are not being true to yourself and you will not be grounded.

Owning your feelings is as simple as saying, "Whatever I'm feeling, that's fine." I can almost hear you screaming back at me that you don't like feeling angry, sad, guilty, ashamed, embarrassed, etc. Well, of course you don't like feeling those emotions, but that doesn't mean that it's wrong to feel them – your emotions are trying to help you.

The roles of your negative emotions

Yep, all those horrible, yucky emotions are trying to speak to you, to cause you to take action, to defend yourself, to run away, to scream or to stay home alone avoiding the rest of the world (amongst a thousand other responses). Let's go through the main negative emotions now.

Sadness

If you've ever seen Pixar's glorious film *Inside Out*, you'll perhaps remember that, at the start of the film, the emotion called Joy can easily tell you what her purpose is, as well as the purpose of the characters Disgust, Fear and Anger. But then she says, "I'm not sure what Sadness does".

If you haven't seen yet seen *Inside Out*, then please watch it – it's great! Either way, I'll explain what I am talking about, which the film eventually demonstrates. If something bad happens to you, then you're absolutely 100% allowed to feel sad. Being sad is fine – it's your mind and body asking for help, either from you or from those around you.

Fighting sadness and desperately trying to be happy, when that's really not how you're feeling, means that the sadness doesn't get processed properly. Repressing your sadness normally ends up with it coming out later but worse. By embracing your sadness, accepting and processing it fully, the emotion will pass more quickly and healthily for you. Being sad is okay and can save you.

Anger

> "Anger is an acid that can do more harm to the vessel in which it is stored than to anything on which it is poured."
>
> Mark Twain

This is probably the emotion that people are the least good at owning. I put myself into this category as well, but I am improving all the time as I recognise the importance of owning anger.

Anger arises when we have been wronged, when we have felt frustrated or powerless, or when we have been treated unfairly. There are hundreds of other triggers, depending on anyone's personal situation and experiences. When we feel angry, we might want to scream, "This isn't right, this isn't fair!". We might want to lash out and hurt people who have wronged us – anger can make us want to cause pain because we are in pain.

I now have to make a very important distinction between being angry and owning your anger. If you are acting in anger, then you are making decisions based on the emotions you are currently feeling – you shout, you scream, you hit, you lash out, you say awful things, you make bad decisions, you get in people's faces. In general, anger isn't very helpful at all.

Owning your anger is entirely different. Owning your anger is about recognising that you have had your boundaries trampled on and then stopping to say to yourself, "Hey, I've had my boundaries trampled on – I feel angry".

This is the huge distinction, and owning your anger is a sign of a true Stoic. Having the ability to keep calm and coolly express how much and why someone's actions have angered you is you *owning* your anger. It is so much more powerful than you screaming your face off or becoming physical with someone. If you shout at someone, then they (generally) shout back, which becomes a "who can shout the loudest" match, where all content gets lost.

Taking all the time you need to accept your emotion of anger and what it means to you, and then explaining this to the person who has angered you, is one of the most powerful reactions ever. Anger is a beautiful and indispensable emotion, which really wants to protect you from harm. It just needs to be nurtured properly.

Here's another crucial distinction. Taking time to process your anger, and then being open about how something has made you feel, is completely different from not getting angry at all.

If someone has wronged you, then if you are to have any continued relationship with this person, they need to know that they have angered you. On the other hand, if you choose to repress your anger entirely by not responding, you'll set yourself onto the meek and treacherous path to becoming a human doormat – the sort of person who simply allows others to do things to them without any recompense whatsoever. No one benefits from being a doormat.

Guilt

Hands up if you've ever done something awful – something so bad that your stomach twists itself inside out and backflips over and over until you just want to be sick.

Yep, me too – just like everyone else.

Guilt is a really simple emotion – it is there purely to tell us when we have wronged someone and that we should feel bad about it. We have done something that is normally out of character, or at worst completely against our personal core-value system.

What do we do when guilt rears its head then? We own it.

How do we own guilt, though? As I mentioned, guilt's job is to tell us we've done something that is out of alignment with our core values. It's there to say, "Hey, you messed up – you should feel bad about this". Now, this is much easier said than done but, once guilt has told you that you've messed up (like you hadn't already known it), you can simply thank the guilt for reminding you of this and let it go. It doesn't mean that you're forgiven. It doesn't mean that everything is suddenly okay. But it does mean that you're finished with the guilt part of whatever you've done. Holding onto guilt for any length of time at all does nothing but cause you more hurt.

How to own guilt

- To own guilt, we must "sit" in the feeling of guilt for a little while

- Think about the scenario from which your guilty feelings stem, with all the circumstances, and think about exactly what it is you did and to whom you did it. How did it affect them? How did it affect other people? What consequences did your actions cause? Yes, I know this is really unpleasant to do as I've done this myself, but this is an essential part of the exercise

- Ask yourself if there is anything left for you to learn from the guilt you're feeling. Can the guilt teach you anything else about yourself, your situation, your future – anything?

- If your guilt is communicating anything new to you at all, then listen to it and learn the lesson. Learning the lesson might take time but the important thing here is understanding what needs to be changed and what you need to learn

- If your guilt is just repeating the same tired, old story and messages that you've already been over 1,000 times, then you are done with that guilt. You can literally tell the guilt (out loud if you wish) that you're done with it. And decide to move on

What about the thing that you did to cause the hurt?

I am genuinely hopeful that you have already learnt from this book that we don't have to concern ourselves with things that are outside our control. This includes things that are in the past; without wanting to appear blasé, "What's done is done".

This doesn't mean you are off the hook, though, by any means! We must take the lesson from whatever has happened and use this to actually improve ourselves. Remember how we talked in Chapter 5 about obstacles being opportunities? The same applies here too – use your own mistakes to create personal growth.

What about what we need to do with or for the person we have wronged? Well, you do what is necessary to make it up to them, even if this includes accepting that you can no longer be a part of their life. Show them the lesson you have learnt and make efforts to ensure it doesn't happen again. Once retribution is achieved, however, they don't get to hold that over you anymore and, until you let go of your own guilt, they will be able to hold onto it as well.

> "To err is human; to forgive, divine."
>
> Alexander Pope

What if you've done something that the person who you've wronged doesn't know about – should we keep this from them to protect them from harm and us from shame? Absolutely not – the truth will out. Although we can often feel we are doing the right thing by concealing our wrongdoings, it is always better in the long run to be honest – holding onto guilt, particularly for anything you consider to be badly wrong, can destroy you from the inside out. Give the person you have wronged the chance to be divine.

Remember that you can and will make mistakes, just the same as everyone else. That doesn't make you a terrible person – it makes you human.

Grief

Unfortunately, we're all going to die one day. Between now and that day, people we love will die, people we need will pass, and people we don't even know will leave this world. Death can be expected or unexpected, it can be fast or slow, and it is never a happy occasion. This isn't all intended to depress – it is simply a cold, hard truth about life that at some point death will occur, and we have no way of knowing when that will be.

Stepping away for a second from the Stoic teachings and more towards my own opinion, I firmly believe that there isn't a right or wrong way to grieve. Grief is a very individual process and has to be done in the way that is the most helpful for you, with no judgments made on how anyone else might be grieving for the same person or for anyone else. As long as your "grieving process" isn't harming anyone or impeding their grieving, you aren't doing anything wrong. You are simply reacting in the way that is best for you.

What about how the Stoics suggest we deal with death and grief?

Well, predictably, it is suggested that all the feelings we experience are embraced fully – that we should never hide from them – coming back to the idea that our feelings have to be owned. The Stoics can seem at times to be a little bit obsessed with death, and it could be said that the goal of a true Stoic is to overcome any fear of death.

Once again predictably, Stoics try to use death as an opportunity to not necessarily advance themselves but to orientate themselves correctly. They have a saying when it comes to grief: "memento mori", which translates as "remember death". By making sure we don't forget that we can lose the people we love, we ensure that we are grateful for them in our lives and always act accordingly towards them. Meanwhile, by remembering that our own lives will end one day, we can ensure we don't waste them.

Clearly, any one of us can be taken from this mortal coil at any minute; the Stoics believe this should be a source of inspiration rather than a reason to be sad.

Sometimes when people feel struck with grief, their reaction is to believe that they should assume a whole new approach to life, regardless of longer-term consequences. You are probably already familiar with the saying that you should "live each day as if it were your last", which is often misinterpreted as meaning that you should remove all your inhibitions and do all the things that you've ever wanted to do, because you could die tomorrow. So why not, right?

I believe that it is much more helpful and beneficial to interpret "live each day as if it were your last" as the inspiration to ensure that every day you live your life in the way in which you have decided to lead your life, with your moral compass set correctly and your core beliefs firmly at the heart of every decision that you make.

Grief is one of the most powerful and profound emotions that we can experience. It cannot be ignored, it must be respected, and it must be owned completely. Only by doing these things can you truly continue with your life in the strongest way possible, whilst fully honouring the person or people you have lost.

Be the decision maker

I've spoken about the importance of owning your feelings as well as some of the most helpful ways to deal with feelings when they arise. Being able to get in control of your emotions quickly and logically is an incredibly powerful skill. It puts you in a position to make rational decisions even when facing adversity, pressure and other people who are not in control of their emotions.

You will be in the enviable mental place of being able to make your own decisions in any situation. While you no doubt already make decisions about what you do, I'm talking here about you *logically* making your decisions, not your emotions making your decisions for you. I mentioned earlier how decisions made when emotions are running high rarely lead to a good outcome. That is because those rash decisions usually come at the cost of logic being involved in the process, and logic is always your friend.

YOU need to be the decision maker, not your emotions.

Making decisions when you are feeling particularly sad can lead to short-term happiness, at the expense of something more beneficial in the long term. Anyone rarely (if ever) shows their best face when angry, which can lead to decisions normally resulting in actions/words that are set out to deliberately hurt other people. This leads to unhelpful things being said or done, which then can't be unsaid or undone, leading to feelings of guilt or remorse, which then also have to be processed.

Decisions made when guilt is prominent are often ones that cause pain to ourselves because we feel bad about what we've done, "I've done something wrong and therefore I must be punished for it". Grief is such a hectic emotion that it is very difficult to be sure about any decision – what might seem like the right decision today might feel wrong tomorrow, which is why I'd say that patience is your strongest asset in the face of grief.

Only make decisions when you feel you've definitely thought through them completely logically and when you have reached the position where you feel that you fully own your emotions. That will make you (not your emotions) the decision maker.

Remembering other people are human

To conclude this section, I thought it would be powerful to think again about everything that we have spoken about, but this time from the perspective of the people we are communicating with.

As I mentioned in the "not-allowed thoughts" section in Chapter 6, none of us are emotional mind readers. There is no way that we can know what the people we're talking to are really thinking. We DO, however, know that people don't always mean exactly what they say and that people often do things that we don't quite understand.

There have probably been full books written on this, but I intend to cover what I feel to be the most pertinent sections of this topic.

Not saying what we mean

You've done this, guaranteed. I would probably bet my mortgage on it. You're not feeling that you look your best, and you're not 100% sure about the outfit you bought for an evening you've been looking forward to (and shopping for) for ages. So you turn to your partner and say, "This looks terrible, doesn't it?". Your partner immediately (and possibly too quickly) responds, "No, you look amazing!"

Now, let's look at the intentions behind what you and your partner have both just said. Your question was essentially rhetorical – you were coming from a position of low self-confidence and asking for your partner's opinion, with the specific goal of gaining a polar response. Your partner, meanwhile, wants to make you feel better about yourself while avoiding unnecessary conflict, as well as the potential stress of an unhappy you spending an hour trying on different outfits.

I am not using this example to pass even the slightest hint of judgment – we've all been in the position where we are lacking in confidence and feeling that we need some reassurance. Similarly, we've all been in the other position of paying someone a reassuring compliment without even thinking about what our true opinion is, let alone whether we should honestly express it. We are human.

This is all about emotional intelligence. We can more often than not instinctively appreciate the mental place where someone's comments and/or actions are coming from. We can then understand their intentions in a much more complete way and hence respond accordingly. Taking someone else's unprocessed emotional actions or words and responding to them in a similarly unprocessed way is a sure-fire way to lead to a conflict, which could easily have been avoided.

While the ideal response to the example above feels obvious, especially as we are talking about two people who know and love each other, the situation is not always as straightforward. Clearly, we don't need to overanalyse everything that is ever said to us but, particularly in emotional situations, it is a good idea to consider *why* someone might be saying something as opposed to *what* they are saying. Are they saying something overly hurtful? If so, then they are probably feeling hurt. Are they making wild accusations of wrongdoing? Then perhaps they have done something wrong themselves?

That guy who constantly puts up selfies in the gym – is he really that vain, or is he seeking validation for his hard work that he isn't able to provide himself internally? The girl who only puts photos on her Instagram with cute bear ears on – does she really love the annoying bear filter, or is her self-esteem in a place where the only photo she likes of herself is the one where the viewer's attention is drawn away from her face?

Taking a step back and looking at the bigger picture of someone's situation will tell you volumes more than the words they speak and the actions they take.

Judgment

Society is very quick to judge on things such as the last two examples I gave, usually thinking the absolute worst thing possible to be correct. "That guy is vain" and "That girl is an idiot".

Instead of the two alternative interpretations I gave, it could just as easily be that the guy in question is one of the vainest men in the world. You know what – so what if he is? If he genuinely feels confident enough to put those photos up and honestly not care what anyone thinks, then more power to him.

Maybe that girl really does just love the bear ears and thinks they make her look cute, and doesn't care what anyone thinks. There again – you go, girlfriend!

It could well be that people are judging those two people because they themselves are jealous and don't have the confidence to do either of these things. The bigger truth is that nobody except those two people knows the real motivations for any of their uploads or actions. And it isn't anyone else's place to judge, anyway.

Wouldn't you love to be in the position where you can do what you want, however you like to do it, and upload whatever photo, without having to double- and then triple-check with yourself that it's okay and that you won't get any bad comments, rude emojis or other negative reactions? Feels impossible, right?

Am I in this situation myself? No, not yet. But I'm doing everything I can to get there as soon as I can. Whoever you are, whatever size you are, whatever you look like – the first step in this process is the same. Stop judging people.

"BUT I DON'T JUDGE PEOPLE!", I hear you cry.

Well yes, you do. We all do.

If you have ever made a comparison between yourself and anyone else, then you've judged them. If you've judged them to be better than you then you'll give yourself a reason for them being better, which is more an insult towards yourself than a compliment to them. And if or when you judge yourself to be better than someone else, then it is more than likely that you will make an excuse for your success rather than compliment yourself on any effort you've made to achieve it.

You've placed yourself into a game you can never win.

You can take yourself out of the game by striving not to judge anyone at all any more.

Consider this idea: every single person in the whole world is actually running their own individual race. Therefore, if someone appears a million miles further along than you, it doesn't matter, because your race is a different one – you can't win their race and they can't win your race. They are in first place in their race, and they're also in last place, just the same as you are in your own race. You are the only person who can win your race, so you are the only person you should concentrate on.

It is impossible to make a judgment without making a comparison (and vice versa). By making a comparison, you are judging yourself. So, stop judging altogether.

You will be amazed by the freedom that this allows you. You will be astonished by just how much better you'll be allowing you to feel about yourself. And you will hardly be able to believe just how much better you feel in your own skin.

This all essentially and very conveniently ties in with two of the main areas from the beginning of this book: gratitude and control. Let's assume that you're going to cease judgments on all others from this moment forward and concentrate solely on bettering yourself – not in relation to anyone else and most certainly not *for* anyone else – bettering yourself for you and you alone. In exactly the same way as imagining your own race to be quite separate from anyone else's, you will no longer make any comparison between yourself and other people. You therefore won't feel any criticism of yourself, nor any need to castigate others.

Now, let's think about this in relation to gratitude. Wherever you are, that's where you begin – there's quite simply no other place you can start. Be grateful for every single part of your being. This includes everything you feel you hate about yourself, everything you love and everything in between. Be thankful for absolutely all of it – the chances of you even being born are billions to one, so even being here is a borderline miracle!

Once you are grateful for everything about yourself – and only then – you can consider yourself truly grounded, with 100% gratitude distilled into every part of your life, where the only thing that you desire (in the true meaning of the word) is exactly what you have right now.

When you desire only what you already have, then you have everything you'll ever need. This will place you in the perfect place for you to grow as a person or might even put you into the position where you don't feel you have to change. Imagine being 100% happy with yourself – how wonderful would that be?

We then move onto control. Remembering what we can and can't control at all times is such a powerful tool to have in your mental arsenal; it goes to prove even further how important it is to view everyone's lives as individual races. No one else has influence over your race and you have no influence over their race. You can by all means choose to be an interested observer in the race in which they are competing (against themselves only), but remember always that this is the extent to which your interest and control extend.

Conclusion on remembering we're all human

As humans, we are complex creatures, which is what makes us so fascinating. Without emotions, our lives would perhaps be easier but ultimately pretty uninteresting – it is our emotions, and the feelings and actions that come about as a result of them, which bring about the most incredible moments that life has to offer.

Emotions, as I don't need to tell you, are also part and parcel of the worst parts of life. But being thoroughly grateful for those in our lives whom we might lose, while being completely honest with other people, ourselves and our emotions, will bring us into a beautifully grounded position.

When truly grounded, we can show strength when we need to be strong and also have the strength to show weakness when times feel so bad that we cannot show strength. Emotions help us grow, help us thrive, and protect us and all the other emotions (our own and other people's). Emotions must be treated with utmost respect, always.

Being a Stoic Bride will empower you to:

- Understand the importance of emotions and how vital it is to own them
- Take time to process all your emotions before making important decisions

- Process others' emotions, and respond to what those people mean, not to what they are saying or doing
- Recognise the futility of judging others and the impact any judgment has on you
- Remember that you are human

CHAPTER 8
Storytelling

As humans, we live and thrive through stories. We make up fairy tales to warn of stranger danger (for example, *Little Red Riding Hood*), the consequences of lying (*The Boy Who Cried Wolf*) and why we should always lock our doors to keep out meddling children (*Goldilocks and the Three Bears*). These stories have been crafted with specific purpose and messages, and we're acutely aware of the moral significance of each story as we hear it or recount it to others.

There is a massive difference between fairy tales and the stories we tell about ourselves, both to others and to ourselves.

Our own stories will often omit massively important details in order to make the story more interesting, to put us in a better or worse light, to make us appear as the victim or the hero. This is somewhat similar to the "negative filtering" mentioned earlier in the book, although there are differences.

If we compare the stories you tell with the actual truth, it can make quite compelling reading in terms of the mental environment we are creating for ourselves with these stories. The scary part is that sometimes we don't even know that we are telling ourselves these stories.

Example stories

These are random examples I have plucked out of the air. They aren't true stories about anyone or anything, but hopefully they will help you gain an understanding of where I'm coming from. Maybe one of them will even resonate with you.

STORY: "I got home from a long day at work; I was absolutely exhausted and there was mess literally everywhere. The whole kitchen was just a state; my partner is so lazy – can he not even put a few dishes away?"

FACTS: Your partner had also been at work all day and had then got in and cooked dinner for the both of you, leaving only the mess made from cooking dinner to clear up. Deep down, you know that you've been a bit lax around the house lately and are projecting those feelings onto him.

STORY: "I'm so busy that I simply don't have time to go to the gym / meet with friends / take up a new hobby."

FACTS: You waste one hour a day playing Candy Crush and two hours every night watching inane TV programmes, which you don't even enjoy that much. You have plenty of time; you're only making excuses for not putting the work in.

STORY: "I've tried every single weight loss and exercise regime out there. None of them work for me – it's all down to genetics."

FACTS: You've tried a few diets but haven't yet found one that's sustainable, so any weight loss has been short-lived. You've also joined a gym and started some classes but not yet found one you really enjoy. After gruelling bouts of fitness, you've also rewarded yourself with your favourite high-cal food.

A wedding example

STORY: I just had to get this dress – it was £5,000 and it's absolutely perfect in every way, and from such a gorgeous boutique.

FACTS: Deep down, you preferred the £900 dress from the department store – it was more comfortable and even felt more flattering. However, you just can't believe a £900 dress will be something everyone will be talking about, especially after the Vera Wang wedding ensemble your best friend splashed out on last year. So you've trimmed other areas of the budget so you can be sure to wow your friends with the price and image of this £5,000 dress.

A personal story

Deep breath. More detail here, as there probably will be for any true story that is personal to you.

STORY: "I was really enjoying university, and met a girl who I really liked and got along great with. I was smitten, and it was obvious the feelings were mutual. This was very close to the end of term, shortly before we returned to our respective home towns for Christmas. Suddenly, the girl I had fallen for stopped replying to my messages and answered only one of my calls for the two weeks we were apart.

"When we got back to university, I couldn't wait to see her again – I was so excited and messaged her the day we got back to try and meet up. She responded, saying 'I am not interested in a relationship with anyone. You're a really nice guy and it isn't you, it's me – I know that sounds like a horrible cliché.'

"I was heartbroken and slumped into a deep depression for a couple of years. It was her fault, for breaking my heart."

FACTS: Now that reality is firmly in check, writing this story today – the one I used to tell myself for years after all this happened – makes me realise how untrue and damaging that story was. I told it to doctors, friends, counsellors – anyone who would listen – but the bottom line is that the story really wasn't a true reflection of events.

CHAPTER 8 – STORYTELLING

The heartbreak from that short-lived relationship might have formed the trigger for my depression, but there is no way it could have been the sole cause.

This was, quite simply, the story I told myself to try and make sense of how I was feeling, to try and make some rhyme or reason of my heartbroken state of mind, to try and understand my wounded feelings of rejection and also to remove blame from myself. None of this was done with any deliberate intention on my part – it was my miswired, depressed brain creating a story to fit in with how I felt.

University wasn't going that brilliantly for me, really – I wasn't 100% enjoying my course, and my housing situation was awful, so I was sleeping (badly) on friends' floors for months on end. I'd had a two-night stand and got on amazingly well with a girl who soon after felt no further attraction to me. She therefore didn't respond to my texts and answered only one phone call. When we got back to university, she took her first opportunity to let me down honestly, quickly and maturely – in the best way a 19-year-old probably knew how to.

She didn't do anything wrong.

She didn't cause my depression.

Telling myself the story I told myself and others for the weeks, months and years that followed doubtlessly caused my depression to last longer.

The fallout from my personal story

The story I told myself was very damaging to me. Blaming this girl for my issues, when she had done nothing wrong, let me completely absolve myself of any blame and hence of having to do anything about the state of my mental health.

The story emphasised that someone had done something bad TO me, so why should I be the one to do anything to help myself; it was her fault, right?

Whilst I don't blame myself for telling myself this story, I really, REALLY wish I'd been able to see that I was lying to myself, at massive detriment to my health.

My depression continued for a couple of years, including episodes of self-harm and a suicide attempt, after which I thankfully came to my senses and called an ambulance. It was only when I hit this rock bottom that I began to work on myself properly. That was well over 12 years before I began writing this book.

I really hope my own personal story highlights how dangerous it can be to tell false stories to yourself and to allow yourself to believe them. Whilst your own story and its consequences might not be as severe as my own example, I am sure you will understand how damaging the effects of any negative personal story can be.

The opposite

There are other stories that we tell ourselves, which are the mirror image of the type of story I've laid out above. Stories in which you gloss over how well you've done at something, how you were actually a hero, thereby denying that you in any way deserve praise.

Now, whilst humility can be a wonderful trait to have, there is always room for us actually to stand up and say, "You know what? I was actually awesome today because I did this". Now, those of you who are immediately saying to yourselves "I can't do that – I'd sound like an egomaniac" – I'd put it to you that it's more egotistical to be worried about looking like an egomaniac than just accepting deserved praise from yourself or others. Please think about that for a moment.

Let's throw back quickly to treating yourself like your best friend. If you were telling a story about your best friend's achievement, would you blatantly swerve around any opportunity to praise them, or would you want to aggrandise them with the praise they truly deserve? I think you know the answer to that already.

Don't be a storyteller

You might consider my personal story above to be too extreme, but my hope is that it will demonstrate just how damaging false stories can be, and motivate you to do the exact opposite and be honest with yourself and others.

When you start to tell yourself or someone else a story – one that justifies or explains your reasons for doing something or being a certain way – stop for a moment and check in with reality. Are you genuinely telling the complete truth about the most significant parts? Or are you exaggerating? Are you lying? Are you twisting the facts to fit in with the narrative you are trying to create?

What would be the harm in actually being 100% honest about something that happened? The beauty in being honest is that it is SO easy to remember exactly what happened and how you were feeling at a particular time. I'm sure there aren't many people who (genuinely) have no experience of trying to unweave a web that has been created and becoming tangled up in small untruths, which have likely also led to larger inaccuracies and some trouble in remembering what's been said.

Even more important is that forcing yourself to accept the reality of a situation puts you in a position to admit your mistakes, both to yourself and to others around you. Mistakes are generally thought of as shameful – they illustrate that you have done something wrong, and when you have done something wrong, you automatically feel that you should be laughed at, told off or made to feel stupid.

Please stop for a moment and allow yourself to reframe this whole concept. Mistakes are beautiful and are part of what makes us human. Not only this, but mistakes are also an incredible opportunity for growth and learning (obstacles are opportunities). Also, admitting to someone else that you have made a mistake generally *increases* their respect for you – you've not only had the humility to admit you've done something wrong, but the other person now feels you are more human and altogether a better person for admitting a mistake.

When you make a mistake, don't gloss over it. Simply admit it, then identify why the mistake happened, then work out what you could do better in the future.

> SIDE NOTE: If you're never making mistakes, then you're not trying enough new stuff, which is a mistake in itself!

The same applies to your successes – tell accurate stories about anything you succeed in, for the good of yourself and those around you too. While people are much quicker to forgive and accept mistakes than you probably think, they will also always appreciate hearing a positive success story. (Well, nearly always – if they don't, they're probably not worth your valuable time in the first place.)

Short stories we tell ourselves

The stories we tell ourselves don't have to be as long or as in depth as the story above. In fact, the stories we don't even perceive as stories can be the most damaging. Single lines of throwaway dialogue, which you express in conversation and written messages, will compound issues that you have in your life, without you having the slightest inkling that this is occurring.

TRIGGER WARNING

During the following pages, I will be using the perfect example to clarify this concept: arachnophobia. I won't include grim details or scary descriptions, but if you are triggered by the very name of those eight-legged creatures, please skip to page 229. I do appreciate that some people suffer so badly from arachnophobia that they can't even bear to hear the S-word.

The concept is pretty simple to grasp and you will not be missing out hugely by skipping this part. However, please be as brave as you can – if you can force yourself to read the solid advice that follows, you will likely be helping yourself by taking the first steps in overcoming your phobia.

END OF TRIGGER WARNING

Arachnophobia

You can exchange the heading above and the following description with your own phobia and its respective examples. When dealing with any phobia from a therapeutic point of view, adjusting the single lines of dialogue that my clients told themselves and others was one of the very first – and one of the most important – things that I would tackle.

I've chosen arachnophobia as my main example here because it is one of the most common phobias, and because arachnophobes are the absolute worst offenders (to themselves) in using detrimentally compounding assertions.

Imagine it is September and you log into Facebook; I can practically guarantee that 10% of the posts you see carry photos of spiders, links to articles about spiders, tales of spiders in the house and posts about it being spider season.

And who are making all those posts? People who are afraid of spiders.

Just answer this to yourself quickly: do you think these actions and posts are going to be helpful or unhelpful to those people in overcoming their fear? Hands up – that was a rhetorical question. All that people are doing when posting this sort of stuff is reminding themselves over and over and over again that they are afraid of spiders. And for what purpose?

Do you think they simply can't imagine how dreadful it would be if they and other people forgot they had a phobia? In fact, no one else needs to know about their fear of spiders, and yet they feel the urge to declare their woeful situation to the world, with the added downside that anyone else who is afraid of spiders gets dragged into the mix. It's also very likely they are seeking to validate their phobia – they've already told friends about it, so now they are keen to demonstrate how real their phobia is and what an impact it's having on their life. But anyone who doesn't mind spiders will pay about as much attention to their Facebook post as the one about someone's latest restaurant choices, while placing the spider post will have further validated and strengthened the arachnophobe's own fear.

When people came to see me about phobias, the story was one of two things. Number one, they had a specific event coming up where they'd have to embrace their fear, e.g. a phobia of flying, when they were about to take their first holiday abroad. Or number two, their fear had been getting worse and worse every year, to the point where they could no longer handle it.

The source of fear hadn't changed, only their actions towards it. They'd repeatedly told themselves or others in conversation, "I'm afraid of spiders", "I can't be in the same room as a spider", "I can't sleep if I think there's a spider in the room", etc. They'd repeated those statements year in, year out, and every year their fear had got worse – what a surprise.

Their short stories have served only to exacerbate their fear of spiders.

Let's turn this on its head. Let's think about positive and helpful short stories.

We've all seen countless memes and inspirational quotes about believing in ourselves. These short stories usually tell us to make sure that we tell ourselves we are able to achieve all the things we'd like to achieve, and how much easier it will then be to achieve them. As contrite as these memes might seem, they do hold genuinely solid advice, although people do still tend to find it hard to apply them to their own lives and situations.

Next time you are inspired by anything you read or hear, why not write it down somewhere you'll see it every day. Write it out a hundred times, or keep saying it out loud. Whatever it takes, if you decide that you are going to allow yourself to enjoy the amazing benefits of what inspired you in the first place, you will be significantly more likely to make that positive change in your life.

The power of yet

There's little or no point in having a positive new story, which you intend to keep telling yourself, if you have 0% genuine belief in that story. Your brain will simply reject it, leading to no positive effect on your life.

Starting with small and believable stories is a much more beneficial way to make progress. Let's assume, for instance, that you've been telling yourself the following short story: "I have absolutely no idea where to seat anyone at my wedding breakfast".

Humour me slightly by saying this out loud. If you're reading this somewhere you'll feel daft talking out loud to yourself, stop for a second and repeat it a few times clearly inside your head: "I have absolutely no idea where to seat anyone at my wedding breakfast".

Now, imagine simply adding the word "yet" to the end of the sentence: "I have absolutely no idea where to sit anyone at my wedding breakfast **yet**."

Again, humour me and repeat this out loud, or at least clearly to yourself. Do you notice how much more positive that sentence sounds and feels? Without "yet", it is a statement without any allowance for change. It seems a definite, a fact, something that will never be overcome. By suffixing the sentence with "yet", there is an immediate implication of a solution, one that you're simply not quite aware of at this moment.

There are plenty of other additions you can make, whenever "yet" isn't quite appropriate. Here are some examples of other short stories (with alterations in brackets).

Other time-related tweaks

"I'm too big to fit into my wedding dress (at the moment)."

"I'm too scared even to get on a plane, so I can't plan a honeymoon abroad (until I get some help with my phobia)."

Solution-focused tweaks

"I can't choose between these two photographers (because I don't have enough information about why the second one charges £200 more)."

"I can't decide on the canapés for the drinks reception (because I need more input from my partner on this)."

Conditional tweaks

"I'm never going to get everything organised in time (if I don't ask for some help from my friends)."

"I'm not going to be able to afford that magician everyone raves about (unless I don't book the popcorn stand)."

By taking a second and mentally adding a positive suffix to the end of any statement, your thoughts will be steered towards being able to achieve it. If you don't bother to think of an enabling suffix, you're essentially only having a rant – you're only telling yourself that something is impossible, hence your belief in your ability to do it decreases each and every time the thought comes into your head. These "impossible" things will then tend to get pushed further down your priority list, as your desire to tackle them also decreases. It will thereby become even more stressful to do those jobs – not only will you have left all the hardest things till last, when the pressure of time is at its highest, but you'll have built them up in your mind to feel much more difficult than they really are.

It's time for you to take control – if you are describing something you feel is difficult or impossible, think of a suffix that will make it feel altogether more achievable.

Evolving your short stories

The tweaks suggested above are the first steps towards overcoming the obstacle. Now I'm going to take you through the possible evolution of a short story, until resolution is achieved.

This is similar to the thought-stopping ("STOP!") technique covered earlier, but rather than only catching and stopping a thought, you will instead replace it with a slightly evolved new story.

In brief, you need to start with the first story, then evolve it into the next story. In time, once that next story is set in your mind, you'll start to move on to the next story down, and so on.

"I have absolutely no idea where to seat anyone at my wedding breakfast."

"I have absolutely no idea where to seat anyone at my wedding breakfast yet."

"Okay, I know now who will be on the top table and I'm starting to get an idea of who I want grouped together."

"I know who will be on the top table, I know who I want grouped together and I know which people I want to be sitting on the tables closest to me."

"I know who will be sitting on each table and I'm starting to get an idea of who should be seated next to whom."

"I've nailed my table plan; where's the gin?"

This step-by-step resolution is incredibly helpful. The thought of going from story 1 to story 6 in one single step is the main reason that this initially seems daunting. Taking your brain through these mini-steps in the stories you're telling yourself will make even the most stressful decisions in your wedding planning – and the issues in your life – that much easier to digest, process and overcome.

Conclusion on storytelling

The stories we tell ourselves can be comforting when we're facing a challenge. They can get us much-needed attention and/or sympathy. Or they can portray us as the hero or the villain, depending on how we feel and how we want to be viewed. Unfortunately, though, none of these stories is actually helpful.

When it comes to finding solutions and making progress, the only helpful stories are the ones dripping with honesty, warts and all, revealing all your successes and your mistakes. These stories are simply true. Own your successes, own your mistakes, and you can learn from both.

Being a Stoic Bride will empower you to:

- Recognise both the negative and the potential positive effects of stories

- Tell stories to yourself and to others that are 100% truthful and helpful

- Own both your successes and your failures

- Constantly learn and improve in just about anything

EPILOGUE
Becoming a Stoic Bride

What started as an idea for a blog post, as part of my regular wedding blog, quickly exploded. Feedback that I received from my initial articles gave me the confidence that people were really willing to gain from my recommendations. Soon after that, I decided to listen to other people's recommendations that I should write a book on this.

Getting married just has to be one of the most exciting times in anyone's life. This is a time when you are making a lifelong commitment and starting on a whole new chapter in your life. I have been incredibly lucky to meet a few brides-to-be who loved every moment of planning their weddings, relishing every new purchase and each new idea and opportunity, while feeling supported and loved by their partner and by all their friends and family.

Those "lucky ones" have at times felt like the tiny minority. I have felt nothing but genuine empathy for all the brides-to-be who have felt overwhelmed by their wedding planning and even by the thought of their wedding day, through no fault of their own. Pressures from society, unrealistic posts on social media, dismal reports of other people's experiences, as well as their own expectations – all these can add up to make wedding planning feel challenging and stressful. But it 100% doesn't need to be.

I hope that you gained inspiration and reassurance from everything I have told you about Stoicism, understanding just how much its principles can help you to improve your life, gain confidence in yourself and become more grounded. I hope that everything in this book will help you throughout your life but, more immediately, that it will enable you to enjoy everything about your wedding, including all the planning.

Integrating Stoicism into your wedding planning and your life isn't a pipe dream. It's a systematic and learnable process that will bring you joy in life, inner peace and appreciation of your beautiful self.

You are the Stoic Bride.

Acknowledgements

This venture has been a labour of love. Whilst I've enjoyed every minute of writing, this book wouldn't have been accomplished without the help of the people listed below. Their support and guidance, and the impact these people have had on me, have enabled me to create this book.

I'm eternally grateful to my partner, Natalie, for believing in all of my crazy schemes and always saying, "Just go for it".

Thanks to Adam Eason, my hypnotherapy teacher, who, apart from being an all-around good bloke and a tremendous therapist, is also the person who introduced me to Stoicism.

To Lucy Hyde, for being an exceptional friend, the strongest person I know and incomparable life coach. Lucy has taught me to drag myself through the worst times of my life and celebrate the best times, and often helped me to apply all these principles to myself. Oh, and thanks for writing the foreword to this book, Lucy.

To my editor, Ilsa, who has helped this to become the best possible book it could be. Your thoughts, ideas and concerns were all invaluable.

To the friends and brides-to-be who read initial drafts and sections – your feedback was immeasurably helpful and inspiring.

Thanks to the most passionate photographer I know, Sadie Osborne, for providing the incredible image for the front cover. The image is of a real bride at a real wedding, not a photoshoot! And to Sarah-Jayne Jefferies (from the front cover) for being an awesome bride and embracing her day to the max!

A big thanks to Steve Rowe, for designing the perfect front cover from the somewhat flaky brief I gave him.

Thank you also to everyone who has taken time to read this book. I genuinely hope that you've found it a source of help and knowledge, and that you're able to apply everything you've learnt in your own life.

Finally, to my friend, Tom Caulfield. I wish I could have imparted all of this knowledge to you and been able to help you through your darkest hours. You are missed.

For more about the author

chrispiercymagic.co.uk

Facebook: facebook.com/CPMagic

Instagram: @chrispiercymagic

Listen to his wedding-planning podcast: search for "Yes to I do" wherever you stream your music

Printed in Poland
by Amazon Fulfillment
Poland Sp. z o.o., Wrocław